THE BRITANNICA GUIDE TO THE SOCIAL SCIENCES

PSYCHOLOGY

EDITED BY
ELISA PETERS and
HOPE LOURIE KILLCOYNE

Britannica
Educational Publishing

IN ASSOCIATION WITH

ROSEN
EDUCATIONAL SERVICES

Published in 2016 by Britannica Educational Publishing (a trademark of Encyclopædia Britannica, Inc.) in association with The Rosen Publishing Group, Inc.
29 East 21st Street, New York, NY 10010

Distributed exclusively by Rosen Publishing.
To see additional Britannica Educational Publishing titles, go to rosenpublishing.com.

First Edition

Britannica Educational Publishing
J.E. Luebering: Director, Core Reference Group
Anthony L. Green: Editor, Compton's by Britannica

Rosen Publishing
Amelie von Zumbusch: Editor
Nelson Sá: Art Director
Brian Garvey: Designer
Cindy Reiman: Photography Manager
Karen Huang: Photo Researcher

Library of Congress Cataloging-in-Publication Data

Names: Peters, Elisa, editor. | Killcoyne, Hope Lourie, editor.
Title: Psychology / Elisa Peters and Hope Lourie Killcoyne, editors.
Description: New York, NY : Rosen Publishing, 2016. | Series: The Britannica
 guide to the social sciences | Audience: Grade 9–12. | Includes
 bibliographical references and index.
Identifiers: LCCN 2015035481 | ISBN 9781622755523 (library bound)
Subjects: LCSH: Psychology—Juvenile literature.
Classification: LCC BF149.5 .P48 2016 | DDC 150—dc23
LC record available at http://lccn.loc.gov/2015035481

Manufactured in the United States of America

Photo Credits: Cover, p. 1 marigold_88/iStock/Thinkstock; p. vii Tetra Images/Getty Images; p. xi Lewis J Merrim/Science Source/Getty Images; p. 1 Science Source; p. 3 Library of Congress, Washington, D.C. (LC-USZ62-94957); p. 7 Kris Timken/Blend Images/Getty Images; p. 11 Steger-photo/Photolibrary/Getty Images; p. 16 Juan Mabromata/AFP/Getty Images; p. 18 Joe Wrinn/The LIFE Images Collection/Getty Images; p. 23 Acc. 90-105 – Science Service Records, 1920s-1970s, Smithsonian Institution Archives; p. 27 Encyclopaedia Britannica, Inc.; p. 34 Map data © 2015 Google; p. 37 © AP Images; p. 42 Vital Pictures/Stone/Getty Images; p. 46 Hero Images/Getty Images; p. 49 ColorBlind Images/Iconica/Getty Images; p. 55 John E Marriott/All Canada Photos/Getty Images; pp. 62–63 Dan Porges/Archive Photos/Getty Images; p. 70 © Gina Sanders/Fotolia; p. 72 Tuan Tran/Moment Select/Getty Images; p. 77 Santi Visalli/Archive Photos/Getty Images; p. 86 Ariel Skelley/Blend Images/Getty Images; p. 88 oliveromg/Shutterstock.com; p. 93 Will & Deni Mcintyre/Science Source/Getty Images; p. 95 Lori Adamski Peek/The Image Bank/Getty Images; p. 100 ullstein bild/Getty Images; p. 104 Courtesy of Clark University, Worchester, Massachusetts; p. 108 Mary Evans/Sigmund Freud Copyrights (courtesy of W.E. Freud); p. 115 Imagno/Hulton Archive/Getty Images; p. 119 Paul Popper/Popperfoto/Getty Images; p. 129 Bill Anderson/Science Source/Getty Images; p. 132 Jon Erikson/Science Source

CONTENTS

vii

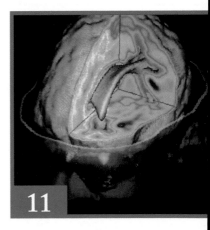

11

16

55

72

86

108

119

132

The study of the way people think and behave is called psychology. The discipline of psychology is broadly divisible into two parts: a large profession of practitioners and a smaller but growing science of mind, brain, and social behaviour. Psychology addresses itself to many of the most basic elements of human mental and emotional life, including concepts, thought, and memory, as well as to complex phenomena such as personality.

The field of psychology has a number of subdisciplines devoted to the study of the different levels and contexts of human thought and behaviour. Social psychology, for example, deals with human thought and action in a social context, while physiological psychology is concerned with thought and behaviour at the level of neurology. Psychology is also an interdisciplinary science. Social psychology, for example, involves both sociology and anthropology, while physiological psychology builds on the techniques and methods of neurology and physiology.

Physiological psychology is concerned with the neurological and physiological events that underlie human thought and action. Some physiological psychologists attempt to map mental phenomena or functioning to various parts of the brain. Others study both the transmission of electrical information in the brain and the neurotransmitters that facilitate or inhibit such transmissions. Physiological psychologists also study the effects of drugs on human behaviour.

Social psychology looks into all facets of human social interaction. Among the problems studied by social psychologists are such matters as the development of friendship, the nature of romantic attachment, and the relative effectiveness of cooperation and competition on achievement. In recent years social psychology has included the study of how people attribute causes to others' (or their own) behaviour. Attribution theory recognizes that psychological perceptions of events do not always correspond to objective reality.

The study of conditioning and learning examines how experience modifies thought and behaviour. Initially devoted to the investigation

Clinical psychologists treat patients who are suffering from mental or emotional problems.

of principles of learning among all species, the field now includes specific types of learning for different species. Other areas of interest include maladaptive learning, such as learned helplessness, and learning in traditional settings such as the classroom and the workplace.

Cognitive psychology encompasses the study of thinking, concept formation, and problem solving. Work in this field has been much influenced and aided by the use of computers. Computers are used to present problems and tasks to subjects and to model thinking and problem-solving processes. The impact of computers on cognitive psychology is also evident in the theories used to describe human thought. For example, such terms as *short-term memory* and *long-term memory* parallel the two types of memory that are available on computers.

Abnormal psychology is the study of maladaptive behaviours. Such behaviours range from simple habit disorders (thumb sucking, nail biting), to addictions (alcohol, gambling and so on) to the most severe mental disturbances (psychoses). Abnormal psychology investigates the causes and dynamics of mental and behavioural disorders and tests the effectiveness of various treatments. There are many different theories of abnormality and treatment. They include Freudian psychoanalysis, non-Freudian psychodynamics, Gestalt psychology, cognitive behaviour therapy, humanistic psychology, and transactional analysis.

Experimental psychology encompasses many different fields of psychology that employ experimental procedures. Traditionally it has been regarded as the study of the basic sensory mechanisms: vision, hearing, taste, touch, and smell. The classical problems of experimental psychology are determining reaction times and reaction thresholds (the amount of stimulation needed to produce a response for any given sense) as well as developing psychological scales for physical stimuli, called psychophysics. Hot and cold, for example, are psychological scalings of temperature stimuli for which such physical measures as degrees Fahrenheit provide only physical units. Much experimental psychology today is closely tied to physiological psychology.

Developmental psychology is concerned with the growth and development of individuals. Originally focused on children, the field has expanded to include people in every age group. Developmental psychologists explore changes associated with mental, social, and emotional development. They also look at the evolution of friendships and parent-child relationships. How children learn, both in and outside school, is another focus of developmental research.

Clinical psychology has undergone rapid growth in recent years and is now the largest subdiscipline within psychology. Clinical psychologists work in hospitals, clinics, and private practice. Their main concerns are the diagnoses and treatment of learning and emotional problems. Many conduct psychological research along with their applied work.

Psychology was recognized as a scientific discipline in the late 19th century. Since the 1950s, there has been much interest in applied psychology, including applications within the various fields and branches. For example, applied child development draws on child development theory and research to develop practical methods and strategies of child rearing and education. Some psychologists in applied child development are concerned with such social issues as the effect of out-of-home care on the development of infants and young children. Others have focused on the effects of different environments on children's health and development.

Because it is an interdisciplinary science, psychology is affected by trends in other disciplines. Discoveries in biology, biochemistry, sociology, and anthropology directly affect psychological research.

Since it overlaps with so many other disciplines, psychology's methods are as varied as the problems that it attempts to investigate. In general, the methods range from simple observation to rigorous experimentation. The use of observation is appropriate in early phases of investigation, when the basic issues and parameters of a problem are not well-known. Experimentation is often the last stage of investigation, when the variables involved are understood well enough to permit quantification and measurement.

Naturalistic methods are often used in child psychology. To determine the frequency with which boys and girls engage in aggressive play in preschool, for example, two different observational methods might be used. In one, called time sampling, the children are observed on a regular basis for a fixed time interval. In another method, episode sampling, the children are observed when engaged in a particular activity, such as block play.

Another tool of psychology is the questionnaire, which may be used to ask subjects about their beliefs, attitudes, childhood experiences, or food and clothing preferences, among many other topics. In order to obtain accurate results, questions must be stated clearly. They must also be varied in order that the subject will not lose interest and begin responding in a routine way, without trying to understand and answer each question. Because subjects are frequently influenced in their responses by what they believe is socially acceptable, questionnaires must also be adjusted to compensate for this tendency.

Testing is perhaps the most widely used method within psychology. Individual and group tests are used to assess intelligence, aptitudes, achievement, interests, and personality. Intelligence tests consist of items that have been pretested on large groups of subjects at different age levels, referred to as the norm group. The responses of the norm group are used to scale the test items according to difficulty. An item passed by 75 percent of the seven-year-old norm group, for example, might be placed at the seven-year level.

Once the items of a test have been scaled, the test can be used to assess intelligence individually or in groups. In some intelligence tests items are scaled by age, and each item answered correctly adds two months to the score. The Stanford-Binet intelligence scale is an example of this kind of test. A child's intelligence quotient (IQ) is derived from the child's test score in years and months, also called mental age (MA), and the child's chronological age (CA). The formula used to determine IQ is $MA/CA \times 100 = IQ$. In other tests, such as the Wechsler intelligence scales, the score is recorded in points rather than in months. A subject of average ability receives a score of 100.

Achievement tests are designed to measure the level of a subject's achievement in a particular discipline. Interest inventories assess the breadth and depth of the subject's interests. Personality tests are usually designed to give a picture of the subject's major personality traits and orientations. They are divided into objective and projective personality tests. In objective tests, subjects can control what they choose to reveal about themselves, whereas in projective tests, the subjects are unable to control what is revealed. Responses to projective tests must be interpreted to be fully understood, and the ability to make such an interpretation takes training and experience.

The ideal method of study in science is experimentation. In an

Rorschach inkblot tests, like the one this boy is taking, were developed by the Swiss psychiatrist Hermann Rorschach. This is a psychological test in which one's perceptions of various inkblots are recorded and interpreted by an analyst, with the results, theoretically, yielding insights into one's personality and cognition.

experiment the investigator has control over one or more independent variables and designs the study to determine the effect of the independent variables upon a dependent variable. Critical to an experiment are another set of factors called control variables. These are held constant so that they will not influence the effect of the independent variables upon the dependent variable.

An important component of most psychological methods is statistics. Through the use of statistics the experimenter is able to determine the likelihood that the results of an experiment occurred by chance. Statistics provides both a method of designing experiments and a means of assuring that quantitative results are statistically significant—that is, not likely to have occurred by chance in one of 100 or 1,000 cases.

The astonishing growth in computational power that began in the final decades of the 20th century transformed methods of data analysis in psychology. More-flexible and more-powerful general linear models and mixed models became available. Similarly, for nonexperimental data, multiple regression analysis began to be augmented by structural equation models that allow for chains and webs of interrelationships and for analysis of extremely complex data. The availability of free, fast, and flexible software also began to change teaching in the measurement area.

Many tests are now computerized. Subjects respond on a keyboard to questions presented on a computer screen. This approach allows for immediate scoring and processing. With computers it is also possible to compare a subject's response pattern to that of many others. As a result, immediate and accurate diagnoses are readily available. Computers have also made psychological research more efficient and effective. With the aid of computer programs, the presentation of stimuli is more controllable than in the past. Computer programs also make it possible to deal with more variables, and with more-complex variables, than was the case when statistical analysis was limited to calculators.

CHAPTER ONE

PSYCHOLOGY: EARLY HISTORY TO THE PRESENT

I n Western culture, contributors to the development of psychology came from many areas, beginning with philosophers such as Aristotle and Plato. Hippocrates phi-

losophized about basic human temperaments such as phlegmatic (even-tempered), sanguine (confident), choleric (hot-tempered), and melancholic (sad). Informed by the biology of his time, he speculated that physical qualities, such as yellow bile or too much blood, might underlie differences in temperament. Aristotle postulated the brain to be the seat of the rational human mind, and in the 17th century, Descartes argued that the mind gives people the capacities for thought and consciousness: the mind "decides" and the body carries out the decision—a dualistic mind/body split that modern psychological science is still

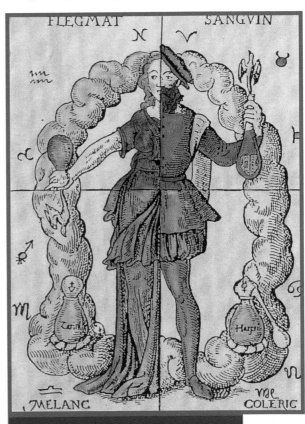

This 16th-century image illustrates (*clockwise from top left*) phlegmatic, sanguine, choleric, and melancholic temperaments.

working to overcome. Two researchers who helped to found psychology as a formal discipline and science in the late 19th century were Wilhelm Wundt in Germany and William James in the United States. James's *The Principles of Psychology* (1890) defined psychology as the science of mental life and provided insightful discussions of topics and challenges for a science of psychology that anticipated much of the field's research agenda a century later.

BEHAVIOURISM

During the first half of the 20th century, behaviourism dominated most of American academic psychology. In 1913 John B. Watson, one of the influential founders of behaviourism, urged reliance only on objective measurable actions and conditions, removing the study of consciousness from psychology. He argued that psychology as a science must deal exclusively with directly observable behaviour in lower animals as well as humans, emphasized the importance of rewarding only desired behaviours in child rearing, and drew on principles of learning through classical conditioning (based on studies with dogs by the Russian physiologist Ivan Pavlov and thus known as Pavlovian conditioning). In the United States most university psychology departments became devoted to turning psychology away from philosophy and into a rigorous empirical science.

Behaviourists in university settings conducted experiments on the conditions controlling learning and "shaping" behaviour through reinforcement, usually working with laboratory animals such as rats and pigeons. American psychologist B.F. Skinner and his followers explicitly excluded mental life, viewing the human mind as an impenetrable "black box," open to only conjecture and speculative fictions. Their work showed that social behaviour is readily influenced by manipulating specific contingencies and by changing the consequences or reinforcement (rewards) to which behaviour leads in different situations. Changes in those consequences can modify behaviour in predictable stimulus-response (S-R) patterns. Likewise, a wide range of emotions, both positive and negative, may be acquired through processes of conditioning and can be modified by applying the same principles.

FREUD AND HIS FOLLOWERS

Concurrently, in a curious juxtaposition, the psychoanalytic theories and therapeutic practices developed by the Vienna-trained physician Sigmund Freud and his many disciples—beginning early in the 20th century and enduring for many decades—were upsetting the view of human nature as a rational entity. Freudian theory made reason secondary: for Freud, the unconscious and its often socially unacceptable irrational motives and desires, particularly the sexual and aggres-

Freud, front left, attended this 1909 conference with (*clockwise*) A.A. Brill, Ernest Jones, Sandor Ferenczi, Carl Jung, and G. Stanley Hall.

sive, were the driving force underlying much of human behaviour and mental illness and symptom formation. Making the unconscious conscious became the therapeutic goal of clinicians working within this framework.

THE UNCONSCIOUS

Also called the subconscious, the unconscious is the complex array of mental activities within an individual that proceed without his or her awareness. Sigmund Freud, the founder of psychoanalysis, stated that such unconscious processes may affect a person's behaviour even though he or she cannot report on them. Freud and his followers argued that dreams and slips of the tongue were really concealed examples of unconscious content too threatening to be confronted directly.

Some theorists denied the role of unconscious processes, defining psychology as the study of conscious states. Yet, the existence of unconscious mental activities is well established and continues to be an important concept in modern psychiatry.

Freud distinguished among different levels of consciousness. Activities within the immediate field of awareness he termed conscious; e.g., reading this book is a conscious activity. The retention of data easily brought to awareness is a preconscious activity; for example, one may not be thinking (conscious) of her address but readily recalls it when asked. Data that cannot be recalled with effort at a specific time but that later may be remembered are retained on an unconscious level. For example, under ordinary conditions a person may be unconscious of ever having been locked in a closet as a child; yet under hypnosis he may recall the experience vividly.

Freud proposed that much of what humans feel, think, and do is outside awareness, self-defensive in its motivations, and unconsciously determined. Much of it also reflects conflicts grounded in early childhood that play out in complex patterns of seemingly paradoxical behaviours and symptoms. His followers, the ego psychologists, emphasized the importance of the higher-order functions and cognitive processes (e.g., competence motivation, self-regulatory abilities) as well as the individual's psychological defense mechanisms. They also shifted their focus to the roles of interpersonal relations and of secure attachment in mental health and adaptive functioning, and they pioneered the analysis of these processes in the clinical setting.

AFTER WORLD WAR II

After World War II, American psychology, particularly clinical psychology, grew into a substantial field in its own right partly in response to the needs of returning veterans. The growth of psychology as a science was stimulated further by Russia's launching of the satellite Sputnik in 1957 and the opening of the Russian-American space race to the Moon. As part of this race, the U.S. government fueled the growth of science. For the first time, massive federal funding became available, both to support behavioral research and to enable graduate training. Psychology became both a thriving profession of practitioners and a scientific discipline that investigated all aspects of human social behaviour, child development, and individual differences, as well as the areas of animal psychology, sensation, perception, memory, and learning.

Training in clinical psychology was heavily influenced by Freudian psychology and its offshoots. But some clinical researchers, working with both normal and disturbed populations, began to develop and apply methods focusing on the learning conditions that influence and control social behaviour. This behaviour therapy movement analyzed problematic behaviours (e.g., aggressiveness, bizarre speech patterns, smoking, fear responses) in terms of the observable events and conditions that seem to influence the person's problematic behaviour. Behavioral approaches led to innovations for therapy by working to modify problematic behaviour not through insight, awareness, or the uncovering of unconscious motivations, but by addressing the behaviour itself.

Behaviourists attempted to modify the maladaptive behaviour directly, examining the conditions controlling the individual's current problems, not their possible historical roots. They also intended to show that such efforts can be successful without the symptom substitution that Freudian theory predicted. Freudians believed that removing the troubling behaviour directly would be followed by new and worse problems. Behaviour therapists showed that this is not necessarily the case.

To begin exploring the role of genetics in personality and social development, psychologists compared the similarity in personality shown by people who share the same genes and/or the same environment. Twin studies compared monozygotic (identical) as opposed to dizygotic (fraternal) twins, raised either in the same or in different environments. Overall, these studies demonstrated the important role of heredity in a wide range of human characteristics and traits, such as those of the introvert and extravert, and indicated that the biological-genetic influence was far greater than early behaviourism had assumed. At the same time, it also became clear that how such dispositions are expressed in behaviour depends importantly on interactions with the environment in the course of development, beginning in utero.

THE IMPACT OF THE COGNITIVE REVOLUTION

By the early 1960s the relevance of the Skinnerian approach for understanding complex mental processes was seriously questioned. American linguist Noam Chomsky's critical review of Skinner's theory of "verbal

Studies of identical twins, like these boys, have given us a greater understanding of genetics and heredity.

behaviour" in 1959 showed that it could not properly account for human language acquisition. It was one of several triggers for a paradigm shift that by the mid-1960s became the "cognitive revolution," which compellingly argued against behaviourism and led to the development of cognitive science. In conjunction with concurrent analyses and advances in areas from computer science and artificial intelligence to neuroscience, genetics, and applications of evolutionary theory, the scientific study of the mind and mental activity quickly became the foundation for much of the evolving new psychological science in the 21st century.

Psychological scientists demonstrated that organisms have pre-wired dispositions and that human brains are distinctively prepared for diverse mental activities, from language acquisition to mathematics, space perception, thinking, and memory. They also developed and tested diverse theoretical models for conceptualizing mental representations in complex information processing conducted at multiple levels of awareness. They asked such questions as: How does the individual's stored knowledge give rise to the patterns or networks of mental representations activated at a particular time? How is memory organized? In a related direction, the analysis of visual perception took increasing account of how the features of the environment (e.g., the objects, places, and other animals in one's world) provide information, the perception of which is vital for the organism's survival. Consequently, information about the possibilities and dangers of the environment, on the one side, and the animal's dispositions and adaptation efforts, on the other, become inseparable: their interactions become the focus of research and theory building.

Concurrently, to investigate personality, individual differences, and social behaviour, a number of theorists made learning theories both more social (interpersonal) and more cognitive. They moved far beyond the earlier conditioning and reward-and-punishment principles, focusing on how a person's characteristics interact with situational opportunities and demands. Research demonstrated the importance of learning through observation from real and symbolic models, showing that it occurs spontaneously and cognitively without requiring any direct reinforcement. Likewise, studies of the development of self-control and the ability to delay gratification in young children showed that how the situation and the temptations are cognitively appraised is crucially important: when the appraisal changes, so does the behaviour. Thus, the focus shifted from reinforcement and "stimulus control" to the mental mechanisms that enable self-control.

Traditional personality trait taxonomies continued to describe individuals and types using such terms as *introversion-extraversion* and *sociable-hostile*, based on broad trait ratings. In new directions, consistent with developments in cognitive science and social psychology, individual differences were reconceptualized in terms of cognitive social variables, such as people's constructs (encoding of information), personal goals and beliefs, and competencies and skills. Research examined the nature of the consistencies and variability that characterize individuals distinctively across situations and over time and began to identify how different types of individuals respond to different types of psychological situations. The often-surprising findings led to new models of cognitive and affective information-processing systems, designed to account for them.

In clinical applications, cognitive-behaviour therapy (CBT) was developed. CBT focuses on identifying and changing negative, inaccurate, or otherwise maladaptive beliefs and thought patterns through a combination of cognitive and behaviour therapy. It helps people to change how they think and feel about themselves and others. In time, these cognitive-behavioral treatment innovations, often supplemented with medications, were shown to be useful for treating diverse problems, including disabling fears, self-control difficulties, addictions, and depression.

In social psychology, beginning in the early 1970s, social cognition—how people process social information about other people and the self—became a major area of study. Research focused on such topics as the nature and functions of self-concepts and self-esteem; cultural differences in information processing; interpersonal relations and social communication; attitudes and social influence processes; altruism, aggression, and obedience; motivation, emotion, planning, and self-regulation; and the influence of people's dispositions and characteristics on their dealings with different types of situations and experiences. Recognizing that much information processing occurs at levels below awareness and proceeds automatically, research turned to the effects of subliminal (below awareness) stimuli on the activation of diverse kinds of mental representations, emotions, and social behaviours. Research at the intersection of social cognition and health psychology began to examine how people's beliefs, positive illusions, expectations, and self-regulatory abilities may help them deal with diverse traumas and threats

9

SELF-ESTEEM

Self-esteem is a sense of personal worth and ability that is fundamental to an individual's identity. Family relationships during childhood are believed to play a crucial role in its development. Parents may foster self-esteem by expressing affection and support for the child as well as by helping the child set realistic goals for achievement instead of imposing unreachably high standards. German-born American psychoanalyst Karen Horney asserted that low self-esteem leads to the development of a personality that excessively craves approval and affection and exhibits an extreme desire for personal achievement. According to Austrian psychiatrist Alfred Adler's theory of personality, low self-esteem leads people to strive to overcome their perceived inferiorities and to develop strengths or talents in compensation.

to their health and the stress that arises when trying to cope with diseases such as HIV/AIDS and cancer. Working with a variety of animal species, from mice and birds to higher mammals such as apes, researchers investigated social communication and diverse social behaviours, psychological characteristics, cognitive abilities, and emotions, searching for similarities and differences in comparison with humans.

In developmental psychology, investigators identified and analyzed with increasing precision the diverse perceptual, cognitive, and numerical abilities of infants and traced their developmental course, while others focused on life-span development and mental and behavioral changes in the aging process. Developmental research provided clear evidence that humans, rather than entering the world with a mental blank slate, are extensively prepared for all sorts of cognitive and skill development. Research also has yielded equally impressive evidence for the plasticity of the human brain and the possibilities for change in the course of development.

LINKING MIND, BRAIN, AND BEHAVIOUR

Late in the 20th century, methods for observing the activity of the living brain were developed that made it possible to explore links between what the brain is doing and psychological phenomena, thus opening a window into the relationship between the mind, brain, and behaviour. The functioning of the brain enables everything one does, feels, and knows. To examine brain activity, functional magnetic resonance imaging (fMRI) is used to measure the magnetic fields created by the functioning nerve cells in the brain, detecting changes in blood flow. With the aid of computers, this information can be translated into images, which virtually "light up" the amount of activity in different areas of the brain as the person performs mental tasks and experiences different kinds of perceptions, images, thoughts, and emotions. They thus allow a much more precise and detailed analysis of the links between activity in the brain and the mental state a person experiences while responding to different

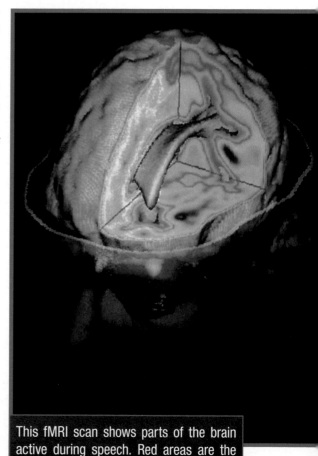

This fMRI scan shows parts of the brain active during speech. Red areas are the most active, followed by yellow.

types of stimuli and generating different thoughts and emotions. These can range, for example, from thoughts and images about what one fears and dreads to those directed at what one craves the most. The result of this technology is a virtual revolution for work that uses the biological level of neural activity to address questions that are of core interest for psychologists working in almost all areas of the discipline.

SOCIAL COGNITIVE NEUROSCIENCE

The advances described above led to the development in the early years of the 21st century of a new, highly popular field: social cognitive neuroscience (SCN). This interdisciplinary field asks questions about topics traditionally of interest to social psychologists, such as person perception, attitude change, and emotion regulation. It does so by using methods traditionally employed by cognitive neuroscientists, such as functional brain imaging and neuropsychological patient analysis. By integrating the theories and methods of its parent disciplines, SCN tries to understand the interactions between social behaviour, cognition, and brain mechanisms.

EPIGENETICS

The term *epigenetic* is used to describe the dynamic interplay between genes and the environment during the course of development. The study of epigenetics highlights the complex nature of the relationship between the organism's genetic code, or genome, and the organism's directly observable physical and psychological manifestations and behaviours. In contemporary use, the term refers to efforts to explain individual differences in physical as well as behavioral traits (e.g., hostility-aggression) in terms of the molecular mechanisms that affect the activity of genes, essentially turning on some genes and turning off others.

Epigenetic regulation of gene activity plays a critical role in the process of development, influencing the organism's psychological and behavioral expressions. Thus, while the genome provides the possibilities, the environment determines which genes become activated. In the early 21st century there emerged evidence for the important role of the environment (e.g., in maternal behaviour with the newborn) in shaping the activity of genes. Epigenetic factors may serve as a critical biological link between the experiences of an individual and subsequent individual differences in brain and behaviour, both within and across generations. Epigenetic research points to the pathways through which environmental influence and psychological experiences may be transformed and transmitted at the biological level. It thus provides another route for the increasingly deep analysis of mind-brain-behaviour links at multiple levels of analysis, from the psychological to the biological.

THE EVOLVING SCOPE AND STRUCTURE OF PSYCHOLOGICAL SCIENCE

The discoveries and advances of psychological science keep expanding its scope and tools and changing its structure and organization. For most of the 20th century, psychological science consisted of a variety of specialized subfields with little interconnection. They ranged from clinical psychology to the study of individual differences and personality, to social psychology, to industrial-organizational psychology, to community psychology, to the experimental study of such basic processes as memory, thinking, perception and sensation, to animal behaviour, and to physiological psychology. In larger academic psychology departments, the list got longer. The various subfields, each with its own distinct history and specialized mission, usually were bundled together within academic departments, essentially a loose federation of unrelated disciplines, each with its own training program and research agenda. Late in the 20th century this situation began to change, fueled in part by the rapid growth of developments in cognitive science and social cognitive neuroscience, including the discovery of new methods for studying cognition, emotion, the brain, and genetic influences on mind and behaviour.

In the early years of the 21st century, psychology became an increasingly integrative science at the intersection or hub of diverse other disciplines, from biology, neurology, and economics to sociology and anthropology. For example, stimulated by the work of two Israeli-born psychologists, Amos Tversky and Daniel Kahneman, notably their theory of decision making under risk, new areas developed, including behavioral economics and decision making, often being taught by psychologists in business schools. Likewise, advances in cognitive neuroscience led to the subfield of neuroeconomics.

In another direction, links deepened between psychology and law. This connection reflected new findings in psychology about the nature of human social behaviour, as well as the fallibility of eyewitness testimony in legal trials and the distortions in retrospective memory.

Likewise, with recognition of the role of mental processes and self-care behaviour in the maintenance of health, the fields of behavioral medicine and health psychology emerged. These subfields study links between psychological processes, social behaviour, and health.

At the same time, within psychology, old sub-disciplinary boundaries were crossed more freely. Interdisciplinary teams often work on a common problem using different methods and tools that draw on multiple levels of analysis, from the social to the cognitive and to the biological.

CHAPTER TWO

THE THOUGHT PROCESS

Thought is the covert symbolic response to stimuli that are either intrinsic (arising from within) or extrinsic (arising from the environment). Thought, or thinking, is considered to mediate between inner activity and external stimuli.

In everyday language, the word *thinking* covers several distinct psychological activities. It is sometimes a synonym for "tending to believe," especially with less than full confidence ("I think that it will rain, but I am not sure"). At other times it denotes the degree of attentiveness ("I did it without thinking") or whatever is in consciousness, especially if it refers to something outside the immediate environment ("It made me think of my grandmother"). Psychologists have concentrated on thinking as an intellectual exertion aimed at finding an answer to a question or the solution of a practical problem.

The psychology of thought processes concerns itself with activities similar to those usually attributed to the inventor, the mathematician, or the chess player. Psychologists have not settled on any single definition or characterization of thinking. For some it is a matter of modifying "cognitive structures" (i.e., perceptual representations of the world or parts of the world), while others regard it as internal problem-solving behaviour.

Yet another provisional conception of thinking applies the term to any sequence of covert symbolic responses (i.e., occurrences within the human organism that can serve to represent absent events). If such a sequence is aimed at the solution of a specific problem and fulfills the criteria for reasoning, it is called directed thinking. Reasoning is a process of piecing together the results of two or more distinct previous learning

How players in a chess game make decisions is the sort of subject that cognitive psychologists study.

experiences to produce a new pattern of behaviour. Directed thinking contrasts with other symbolic sequences that have different functions, such as the simple recall (mnemonic thinking) of a chain of past events.

DEVELOPMENTS IN THE STUDY OF THOUGHT

Historically, thinking was associated with conscious experiences, but, as the scientific study of behaviour (e.g., behaviourism) developed within psychology, the limitations of introspection as a source of data became apparent. Thought processes have since been treated as intervening variables or constructs with properties that must be inferred from relations between two sets of observable events. These events are inputs (stimuli, present and past) and outputs (responses, including bodily movements and speech). For many psychologists, such intervening variables serve as aids in making sense of the immensely complicated network of associations between stimulus conditions and responses, the analysis of which otherwise would be prohibitively cumbersome. Others are concerned, rather, with identifying cognitive (or mental) structures that consciously or unconsciously guide a human being's observable behaviour.

ELEMENTS OF THOUGHT

The prominent use of words in thinking ("silent speech") encouraged the belief, especially among behaviourist and neobehaviourist psychologists, that to think is to string together linguistic elements subvocally. Early experiments revealed that thinking is commonly accompanied by electrical activity in the muscles of the thinker's organs of articulation (e.g., in the throat). Through later work with electromyographic equipment, it became apparent that the muscular phenomena are not the actual vehicles of thinking; they merely facilitate the appropriate activities in the brain when an intellectual task is particularly exacting. The identification of thinking with speech was assailed by the Russian psychologist Lev Semyonovich Vygotsky and by the Swiss developmental psychologist Jean Piaget, both of whom observed the origins of human reasoning in children's general ability to assemble nonverbal acts into effective and flexible combinations. These theorists insisted that thinking and speaking arise independently, although they acknowledged the profound interdependence of these functions.

Following different approaches, three scholars—the 19th-century Russian physiologist Ivan Mikhailovich Sechenov; the American founder of behaviourism, John B. Watson; and Piaget—independently arrived at the conclusion that the activities that serve as elements of thinking are internalized or "fractional" versions of motor responses. In other words, the elements are considered to be attenuated or curtailed variants of neuromuscular processes that, if they were not subjected to partial inhibition, would give rise to visible bodily movements.

Sensitive instruments can indeed detect faint activity in various parts of the body other than the organs of speech—e.g., in a person's limbs when movement is thought of or imagined without actually taking place. Recent studies show the existence of a gastric "brain," a set of neural networks in the stomach. Such findings have prompted theories to the effect that people think with the whole body and not only with the brain, or that, in the words of the American psychologist B.F. Skinner, "thought is simply *behaviour*—verbal or nonverbal, covert or overt."

Skinner was an influential exponent of behaviourism.

The logical outcome of these and similar statements was the peripheralist view. Evident in the work of Watson and the American psychologist Clark L. Hull, it held that thinking depends on events in the musculature: these events, known as proprioceptive impulses (i.e., impulses arising in response to physical position, posture, equilibrium, or internal condition), influence subsequent events in the central nervous system, which ultimately interact with external stimuli in guiding further action. There is, however, evidence that thinking is not prevented by administering drugs that suppress all muscular activity. Furthermore, it has been pointed out by researchers such as the American psychologist Karl S. Lashley that thinking, like other more-or-less skilled activities, often proceeds so quickly that there is not enough time for impulses to be transmitted from the central nervous system to a peripheral organ and back again between consecutive steps. So the centralist view—that thinking consists of events confined to the brain (though often accompanied by widespread activity in the rest of the body)—gained ground later in the 20th century. Nevertheless, each of these neural events can be regarded both as a response (to an external stimulus or to an earlier neurally mediated thought or combination of thoughts) and as a stimulus (evoking a subsequent thought or a motor response).

The elements of thinking are classifiable as "symbols" in accordance with the conception of the sign process ("semiotics") that grew out of the work of philosophers (e.g., Charles Sanders Peircc), linguists (e.g., C.K. Ogden and Ivor A. Richards), and psychologists specializing in learning (e.g., Hull, Neal E. Miller, O. Hobart Mowrer, and Charles E. Osgood). The gist of this conception is that a stimulus event x can be regarded as a sign representing (or "standing for") another event y if x evokes some, but not all, of the behaviour (both external and internal) that would have been evoked by y if it had been present. When a stimulus that qualifies as a sign results from the behaviour of an organism for which it acts as a sign, it is called a "symbol." The "stimulus-producing responses" that are said to make up thought processes (as when one thinks of something to eat) are prime examples.

CHILD PSYCHOLOGY

Child psychology, also called child development, is the study of the psychological processes of children and, specifically, how these processes differ from those of adults, how they develop from birth to the end of adolescence, and how and why they differ from one child to the next. The topic is sometimes grouped with infancy, adulthood, and aging under the category of developmental psychology.

As a scientific discipline with a firm empirical basis, child study is of comparatively recent origin. It was initiated in 1840, when Charles Darwin began a record of the growth and development of one of his own children, collecting the data much as if he had been studying an unknown species. A similar, more elaborate study published by German psychophysiologist William Preyer put forth the methods for a series of others. In 1891 American educational psychologist G. Stanley Hall established the *Pedagogical Seminary*, a periodical devoted to child psychology and pedagogy. During the early 20th century, the development of intelligence tests and the establishment of child guidance clinics further defined the field of child psychology.

A number of notable 20th-century psychologists—among them Sigmund Freud, Melanie Klein, and Freud's daughter Anna Freud—dealt with child development chiefly from the psychoanalytic point of view. Perhaps the greatest direct influence on modern child psychology was Jean Piaget of Switzerland. By means of direct observation and interaction, Piaget developed a theory of the acquisition of understanding in children. He described the various stages of learning in childhood and characterized children's perceptions of themselves and of the world at each stage of learning.

The data of child psychology are gathered from a variety of sources. Observations by relatives, teachers, and other adults, as well as the psychologist's direct observation of and interviews with a child (or children), provide much material. In some cases a one-way window or mirror is used so that children are free to interact with their environment or others without knowing that they are being watched. Personality tests, intelligence tests, and experimental methods have also proved useful in understanding child development.

This treatment, favoured by psychologists of the stimulus-response (S-R) or neo-associationist current, contrasts with that of the various cognitivist or neorationalist theories. Rather than regarding the components of thinking as derivatives of verbal or nonverbal motor acts (and thus subject to laws of learning and performance that apply to learned behaviour in general), cognitivists see the components of thinking as unique central processes, governed by principles that are peculiar to them. These theorists attach overriding importance to the so-called structures in which "cognitive" elements are organized, and they tend to see inferences, applications of rules, representations of external reality, and other ingredients of thinking at work in even the simplest forms of learned behaviour.

The school of Gestalt psychology holds the constituents of thinking to be of essentially the same nature as the perceptual patterns that the nervous system constructs out of sensory excitations. After the mid-20th century, analogies with computer operations acquired great currency; in consequence, thinking came to be described in terms of storage, retrieval, and transmission of items of information. The information in question was held to be freely translatable from one "coding" to another without impairing its functions. What came to matter most was how events were combined and what other combinations might have occurred instead.

THE PROCESS OF THOUGHT

According to the classical empiricist-associationist view, the succession of ideas or images in a train of thought is determined by the laws of association. Although additional associative laws were proposed from time to time, two invariably were recognized. The law of association by contiguity states that the sensation or idea of a particular object tends to evoke the idea of something that has often been encountered together with it. The law of association by similarity states that the sensation or idea of a particular object tends to evoke the idea of something that is similar to it. The early behaviourists, beginning with Watson, espoused essentially the same formulation but with some important modifications. For them the elements of the process were conceived not as conscious ideas but as fractional or incipient motor responses, each producing its proprioceptive stimulus. Association by contiguity and similarity were identified by these behaviourists with the Pavlovian principles of conditioning and generalization.

The Würzburg school, under the leadership of the German psychologist and philosopher Oswald Külpe, saw the prototype of directed thinking in the "constrained-association" experiment, in which the subject has to supply a word bearing a specified relation to a stimulus word (e.g., an opposite to an adjective, or the capital of a country). Introspective research led the members of the Würzburg school to conclude that the emergence of the required element depends jointly on the immediately preceding element and on some kind of "determining tendency" such as *Aufgabe* ("awareness of task") or "representation of the goal." The last two factors were held to impart a direction to the thought process and to restrict its content to relevant material. Their role was analogous to that of motivational factors—"drive stimuli," "fractional anticipatory goal responses" in the later neobehaviouristic accounts of reasoning (and of behaviour in general) produced by Hull and his followers.

Hull's theory resembled the earlier "constellation theory" of constrained association developed by German psychologist Georg Elias Müller. Hull held that one particular response will occur and overcome its competitors because it is associated both with the cue stimulus (which may be the immediately preceding thought process or an external event) and with the motivational condition (task, drive stimulus) and is thus evoked with more strength than are elements associated only with the cue stimulus or the motivational condition. Another German psychologist, Otto Selz, countered that in many situations this kind of theory would imply the occurrence of errors as often as correct answers to questions and thus was untenable. Selz contended that response selection depends

Hull, right, was known for his studies on learning and his attempt to give mathematical expression to psychological theory.

rather on a process of "complex completion" that is set in motion by an "anticipatory schema," which includes a representation of both the cue stimulus and the relation that the element to be supplied must bear to the cue stimulus. The correct answer is associated with the schema as a whole and not with its components separately. Selz's complex completion resembles the "eduction of correlates" that the British psychologist Charles E. Spearman saw as a primary constituent of intellectual functioning, its complement being "eduction of relations"—that is, recognition of a relation when two elements are presented.

The determination of each thought element by the whole configuration of factors in the situation and by the network of relations linking them was stressed still more strongly by the Gestalt psychologists in the 1920s and '30s. On the basis of experiments by German psychologist Wolfgang Köhler (on "insightful" problem solving by chimpanzees) and Czech-born psychologist Max Wertheimer and his student Karl Duncker (on human thinking), they pointed out that the solution to a problem commonly requires an unprecedented response or pattern of responses that hardly could be attributed to simple associative reproduction of past behaviour or experiences. For them, the essence of thinking lay in sudden perceptual restructuring or reorganization, akin to the abrupt changes in appearance of an ambiguous visual figure.

The Gestalt theory has had a deep and far-reaching impact, especially in drawing attention to the ability of the thinker to discover creative, innovative ways of coping with situations that differ from any that have been encountered before. This theory, however, has been criticized for underestimating the contribution of prior learning and for not going beyond rudimentary attempts to classify and analyze the structures that it deems so important. Later discussions of the systems in which items of information and intellectual operations are organized have made fuller use of the resources of logic and mathematics. Merely to name them, they include the "psychologic" of Piaget, the computer simulation of human thinking by the American computer scientists Herbert A. Simon and Allen Newell, and extensions of Hull's

INSIGHT

In learning theory, insight is the immediate and clear learning or understanding that takes place without overt trial-and-error testing. Insight occurs in human learning when people recognize relationships (or make novel associations between objects or actions) that can help them solve new problems.

Much of the scientific knowledge concerning insight derives from work on animal behaviour that was conducted by Wolfgang Köhler. In one experiment, Köhler placed a banana outside the cage of a hungry chimpanzee, Sultan, and gave the animal two sticks, each too short for pulling in the food but joinable to make a single stick of sufficient length. Sultan tried unsuccessfully to use each stick, and he even used one stick to push the other along to touch the banana. Later, apparently after having given up, Sultan accidentally joined the sticks, observed the result, and immediately ran with the longer tool to retrieve the banana. When the experiment was repeated, Sultan joined the two sticks and solved the problem immediately. This result, however, is ambiguous, because it appeared that Sultan solved the problem by accident—not through insight.

notion of the "habit-family hierarchy" by Irving Maltzman and Daniel E. Berlyne.

Also important is a growing recognition that the essential components of the thought process, the events that keep it moving in fruitful directions, are not words, images, or other symbols representing stimulus situations; rather, they are the operations that cause each of these representations to be succeeded by the next, in conformity with restrictions imposed by the problem or aim of the moment. In other words, directed thinking can reach a solution only by going through a properly ordered succession of "legitimate steps." These steps might be representations of realizable physicochemical changes, modifications of logical or mathematical formulas that are permitted by rules of inference, or legal moves in a game of chess. This conception of the train of thinking as a sequence of rigorously controlled transformations is buttressed by the theoretical arguments of Sechenov and of Piaget, the results of the Würzburg experiments, and the lessons of computer simulation.

Early in the 20th century, the Swiss psychologist Édouard Claparède and the American philosopher John Dewey both suggested that directed thinking proceeds by "implicit trial-and-error." That is to say, it resembles the process whereby laboratory animals, confronted with a novel problem situation, try out one response after another until they sooner or later hit upon a response that leads to success. In thinking, however, the trials were said to take the form of internal responses (imagined or conceptualized courses of action, directions of symbolic search); once attained, a train of thinking that constitutes a solution frequently can be recognized as such without the necessity of implementation through action and sampling of external consequences. This kind of theory, popular among behaviourists and neobehaviourists, was stoutly opposed by the Gestalt school, whose insight theory emphasized the discovery of a solution as a whole and in a flash.

The divergence between these theories appears, however, to represent a false dichotomy. The protocols of Köhler's chimpanzee experiments and of the rather similar experiments performed later under Pavlov's auspices show that insight typically is preceded by a period of groping and of misguided attempts at a solution that are eventually abandoned. On the other hand, even the trial-and-error behaviour of an animal in a simple selective-learning situation does not consist of a completely blind and random sampling of the behaviour of which the learner is capable. Rather, it consists of responses that very well might have succeeded if the circumstances had been slightly different.

Along with being a pioneering psychologist, Dewey was a philosopher and educator.

Newell, Simon, and the American computer scientist J. Clifford Shaw pointed out the indispensability in creative human thinking, as in its computer simulations, of what they called "heuristics." (A heuristic is an informal principle or procedure used as a method of problem solving.) In terms of both thought and computing, a large number of possibilities may have to be examined, but the search is organized heuristically in such a way that the directions most likely to lead to success are explored first. Means of ensuring that a solution will occur within a reasonable time—certainly much faster than by random hunting—include adoption of successive subgoals and working backward from the final goal (the formula to be proved, the state of affairs to be brought about).

MOTIVATIONAL ASPECTS OF THINKING

The problem to be taken up and the point at which the search for a solution will begin are customarily prescribed by the investigator for a subject participating in an experiment on thinking (or by the programmer for a computer). Thus, prevailing techniques of inquiry in the psychology of thinking have invited neglect of the motivational aspects of thinking. Investigation has barely begun on the conditions that determine when the person will begin to think in preference to some other activity, what he will think about, what direction his thinking will take, and when he will regard his search for a solution as successfully terminated (or abandon it as not worth pursuing further). Although much thinking is aimed at practical ends, special motivational problems are raised by "disinterested" thinking, in which the discovery of an answer to a question is a source of satisfaction in itself.

In the views of the Gestalt school and of the British psychologist Frederic C. Bartlett, the initiation and direction of thinking are governed by recognition of a "disequilibrium" or "gap" in an intellectual structure. Similarly, Piaget's notion of "equilibration" as a process impelling advance from less-equilibrated structures, fraught with uncertainty and inconsistency, toward better-equilibrated structures that overcome these imperfections was introduced to explain the child's progressive intellectual development in general. Piaget's approach may also be applicable to specific episodes of thinking. For computer specialists, the detection of a mismatch between the formula that the program so far has produced and some formula or set of requirements that define a solution is what impels continuation of the search and determines the direction it will follow.

Neobehaviourism (like psychoanalysis) has made much of secondary reward value and stimulus generalization—i.e., the tendency of a stimulus pattern to become a source of satisfaction if it resembles or has frequently accompanied some form of biological gratification. The insufficiency of this kind of explanation becomes apparent, however, when the importance of novelty, surprise, complexity, incongruity, ambiguity, and uncertainty is considered. Inconsistency between beliefs, between items of incoming sensory information, or between one's belief and an item of sensory information evidently can be a source of discomfort impelling a search for resolution through reorganization of belief systems or through selective acquisition of new information.

The motivational effects of such factors began receiving more attention in the middle of the 20th century, mainly because of the pervasive role they were found to perform in exploratory behaviour, play, and aesthetics. Their larger role in all forms of thinking has come to be appreciated and has been studied in relation to curiosity, conflict, and uncertainty.

TYPES OF THINKING

Philosophers and psychologists alike have long realized that thinking is not of a "single piece." There are many different kinds of thinking, and there are various means of categorizing them into a "taxonomy" of thinking skills, but there is no single universally accepted taxonomy. One common approach divides the types of thinking into problem solving and reasoning, but other kinds of thinking, such as judgment and decision making, have been suggested as well.

PROBLEM SOLVING

Problem solving is a systematic search through a range of possible actions in order to reach a predefined goal. It involves two main types of thinking: divergent, in which one tries to generate a diverse assortment of possible alternative solutions to a problem, and convergent, in which one tries to narrow down multiple possibilities to find a single, best answer to a problem. Multiple-choice tests, for example, tend to involve convergent thinking, whereas essay tests typically engage divergent thinking.

THE PROBLEM-SOLVING CYCLE IN THINKING

Many researchers regard the thinking that is done in problem solving as cyclical, in the sense that the output of one set of processes— the solution to a problem—often serves as the input of another—a new problem to be solved. American psychologist Robert J. Sternberg identified seven steps in problem solving, each of which may be illustrated in the simple example of choosing a restaurant:

1. Problem identification. In this step, the individual recognizes the existence of a problem to be solved: he recognizes that he is hungry, that it is dinnertime, and hence that he will need to take some sort of action.
2. Problem definition. In this step, the individual determines the nature of the problem that confronts him. He may

define the problem as that of preparing food, of finding a friend to prepare food, of ordering food to be delivered, or of choosing a restaurant.

3. Resource allocation. Having defined the problem as that of choosing a restaurant, the individual determines the kind and extent of resources to devote to the choice. He may consider how much time to spend in choosing a restaurant, whether to seek suggestions from friends, and whether to consult a restaurant guide.

4. Problem representation. In this step, the individual mentally organizes the information needed to solve the problem. He may decide that he wants a restaurant that meets certain criteria, such as close proximity, reasonable price, a certain cuisine, and good service.

5. Strategy construction. Having decided what criteria to use, the individual must now decide how to combine or prioritize them. If his funds are limited, he might decide that reasonable price is a more important criterion than close proximity, a certain cuisine, or good service.

6. Monitoring. In this step, the individual assesses whether the problem solving is proceeding according to his intentions. If the possible solutions produced by his criteria do not appeal to him, he may decide that the criteria or their relative importance needs to be changed.

7. Evaluation. In this step, the individual evaluates whether the problem solving was successful. Having chosen a restaurant, he may decide after eating whether the meal was acceptable.

This example also illustrates how problem solving can be cyclical rather than linear. For example, once one has chosen a restaurant, one must determine how to get there, what to order, how much to tip, and so on.

STRUCTURES OF PROBLEMS

Psychologists often distinguish between "well-structured" and "ill-structured" problems. Well-structured problems (also called well-defined problems) have clear solution paths: the problem solver is usually able to specify, with relative ease, all the steps that must be taken to reach a solution. The difficulty in such cases, if any, has to do with executing the steps. Most mathematics problems, for example, are well-structured, in the sense that determining what needs to be done is easy, though carrying out the computations needed to reach the solution may be difficult. The problem represented by the question, "What is the shortest driving route from New York City to Boston?" is also well-structured, because anyone seeking a solution can consult a map to answer the question with reasonable accuracy.

Ill-structured problems (also called ill-defined problems) do not have clear solution paths, and in such cases the problem solver usually cannot specify the steps needed to reach a solution. An example of an ill-structured problem is, "How can a lasting peace be achieved between country A and country B?" It is hard to know precisely (or, perhaps, even imprecisely) what steps one would take to solve this problem. Another example is the problem of writing a best-selling novel. No single formula seems to work for everyone. Indeed, if there were such a formula, and if it became widely known, it probably would cease to work (because the efficacy of the formula would be destroyed by its widespread use).

The solution of ill-structured problems often requires insight, which is a distinctive and seemingly sudden understanding of a problem or strategy that contributes toward a solution. Often an insight involves conceptualizing a problem or a strategy in a totally new way. Although insights sometimes seem to arise suddenly, they are usually the necessary result of much prior thought and hard work. Sometimes, when one is attempting to gain an insight but is unsuccessful, the most effective approach is that of "incubation"—laying the problem aside for a while and processing it unconsciously. Psychologists have found that unconscious incubation often facilitates solutions to problems.

ALGORITHMS AND HEURISTICS

Other means of solving problems incorporate procedures associated with mathematics, such as algorithms and heuristics, for both well- and ill-structured problems. Research in problem solving commonly distinguishes between algorithms and heuristics, because each approach solves problems in different ways and with different assurances of success.

A problem-solving algorithm is a procedure that is guaranteed to produce a solution if it is followed strictly. In a well-known example, the "British Museum technique," a person wishes to find an object on display among the vast collections of the British Museum but does not know where the object is located. By pursuing a sequential examination of every object displayed in every room of the museum, the person will eventually find the object, but the approach is likely to consume a considerable amount of time. Thus, the algorithmic approach, though certain to succeed, is often slow.

A problem-solving heuristic is an informal, intuitive, speculative procedure that leads to a solution in some cases but not in others. The fact that the outcome of applying a heuristic is unpredictable means that the strategy can be either more or less effective than using an algorithm. Thus, if one had an idea of where to look for the sought-after object in the British Museum, a great deal of time could be saved by searching heuristically rather than algorithmically. But if one happened to be wrong about the location of the object, one would have to try another heuristic or resort to an algorithm.

Although there are several problem-solving heuristics, a small number tend to be used frequently. They are known as means-ends analysis, working forward, working backward, and generate-and-test.

In means-ends analysis, the problem solver begins by envisioning the end, or ultimate goal, and then determines the best strategy for attaining the goal in his current situation. If, for example, one wished to drive from New York to Boston in the minimum time possible, then, at any given point during the drive, one would choose the route that minimized the time it would take to cover the remaining distance, given traffic conditions, weather conditions, and so on.

In the working-forward approach, as the name implies, the problem solver tries to solve the problem from beginning to end. A trip from New York City to Boston might be planned simply by consulting a map and establishing the shortest route that originates in New York City and ends in Boston. In the working-backward approach, the problem solver starts at the end and works toward the beginning. For example, suppose one is planning a trip from New York City to Paris. One wishes to arrive at one's Parisian hotel. To arrive, one needs to take a taxi from Orly Airport. To arrive at the airport, one needs to fly on an airplane; and so on, back to one's point of origin.

Many times the least systematic of the problem-solving heuristics, the generate-and-test method, involves coming up with alternative courses of action, often in a random fashion, and then determining for each course whether it will solve the problem. In plotting the route from New York City to Boston, one might generate a possible route and see

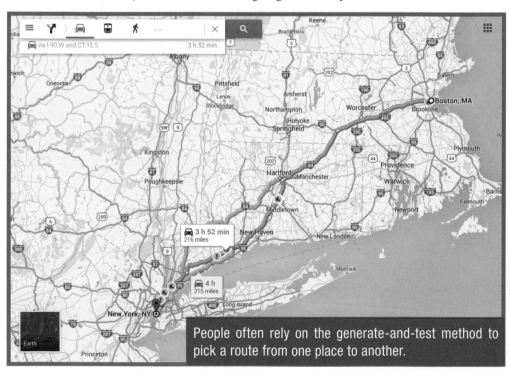

People often rely on the generate-and-test method to pick a route from one place to another.

whether it can get one expeditiously from New York to Boston; if so, one sticks with that route. If not, one finds another route and evaluates it. Eventually, one chooses the route that seems to work best, or at least a route that works. As this example suggests, it is possible to distinguish between an optimizing strategy, which gives one the best path to a solution, and a satisficing strategy, which is the first acceptable solution one generates. The advantage of optimizing is that it yields the best possible strategy; the advantage of satisficing is that it reduces the amount of time and energy involved in planning.

OBSTACLES TO EFFECTIVE THINKING

A better understanding of the processes of thought and problem solving can be gained by identifying factors that tend to prevent effective thinking. Some of the more common obstacles, or blocks, are mental set, functional fixedness, stereotypes, and negative transfer.

A mental set, or "entrenchment," is a frame of mind involving a model that represents a problem, a problem context, or a procedure for problem solving. When problem solvers have an entrenched mental set, they fixate on a strategy that normally works well but does not provide an effective solution to the particular problem at hand. A person can become so used to doing things in a certain way that, when the approach stops working, it is difficult for him or her to switch to a more effective way of doing things.

Functional fixedness is the inability to realize that something known to have a particular use may also be used to perform other functions. When one is faced with a new problem, functional fixedness blocks one's ability to use old tools in novel ways. Overcoming functional fixedness first allowed people to use reshaped coat hangers to get into locked cars, and it is what first allowed thieves to pick simple spring door locks with credit cards.

Another block involves stereotypes. The most common kinds of stereotypes are rationally unsupported generalizations about the putative characteristics of all, or nearly all, members of a given social group. Most people learn many stereotypes during childhood. Once they become accustomed to stereotypical thinking, they may not be able to see individuals or situations for what they are.

Negative transfer occurs when the process of solving an earlier problem makes later problems harder to solve. It is contrasted with positive transfer, which occurs when solving an earlier problem makes it easier to solve a later problem. Learning a foreign language, for example, can either hinder or help the subsequent learning of another language.

EXPERT THINKING AND NOVICE THINKING

Research by the American psychologists Herbert A. Simon, Robert Glaser, and Micheline Chi, among others, has shown that experts and novices think and solve problems in somewhat different ways. These differences explain why experts are more effective than novices in a variety of problem-solving endeavours.

As compared with novices, experts tend to have larger and richer schemata (organized representations of things or events that guide a person's thoughts and actions), and they possess far greater knowledge in specific domains. The schemata of experts are also highly interconnected, meaning that retrieving one piece of information easily leads to the retrieval of another piece. Experts devote proportionately more time to determining how to represent a problem, but they spend proportionately less time in executing solutions. In other words, experts tend to allocate more of their time to the early or preparatory stages of problem solving, whereas novices tend to spend relatively more of their time in the later stages. The thought processes of experts also reveal more complex and sophisticated representations of problems. In terms of heuristics, experts are more likely to use a working-forward

Simon contributed to several fields, including psychology, mathematics, statistics, and operations research.

strategy, whereas novices are more likely to use a working-backward strategy. In addition, experts tend to monitor their problem solving more carefully than do novices, and they are also more successful in reaching appropriate solutions.

REASONING

Reasoning consists of the derivation of inferences or conclusions from a set of premises by means of the application of logical rules or laws. Psychologists as well as philosophers typically distinguish between two main kinds of reasoning: deduction and induction.

DEDUCTION

Deductive reasoning, or deduction, involves analyzing valid forms of argument and drawing out the conclusions implicit in their premises. There are several different forms of deductive reasoning, as used in different forms of reasoning problems.

In conditional reasoning the reasoner must draw a conclusion based on a conditional, or "if...then," proposition. For example, from the conditional proposition "if today is Monday, then I will attend cooking class today" and the categorical (declarative) proposition "today is Monday," one can infer the conclusion, "I will attend cooking class today." In fact, two kinds of valid inference can be drawn from a conditional proposition. In the form of argument known as *modus ponens*, the categorical proposition affirms the antecedent of the conditional, and the conclusion affirms the consequent, as in the example just given. In the form known as *modus tollens*, the categorical proposition denies the consequent of the conditional, and the conclusion denies the antecedent. Thus:

If today is Monday, then I will attend cooking class today. I will not attend cooking class today. Therefore, today is not Monday.

Two other kinds of inference that are sometimes drawn from conditional propositions are not logically justified. In one such fallacy, "affirming the consequent," the categorical proposition affirms the consequent of the conditional, and the conclusion affirms the antecedent, as in the example:

If John is a bachelor, then he is male. John is male. Therefore, John is a bachelor.

In another invalid inference form, "denying the antecedent," the categorical proposition denies the antecedent of the conditional, and the conclusion denies the conclusion of the conditional:

If Othello is a bachelor, then he is male. Othello is not a bachelor. Therefore, Othello is not male.

The invalidity of these inference forms is indicated by the fact that in each case it is possible for the premises of the inference to be true while the conclusion is false.

It is important to realize that in conditional reasoning, and in all forms of deductive reasoning, the validity of an inference does not depend on whether the premises and the conclusion are actually (in the "real world") true or false. All that matters is whether it is possible to conceive of a situation in which the conclusion would be false and all of the premises would be true. Indeed, there are valid inferences in which one or more of the premises and the conclusion are actually false:

Either the current pope is married or he is a divorcé. The current pope is not a divorcé. Therefore, the current pope is married.

This inference is valid because, although the premises and the conclusion are not all true, it is impossible to conceive of a situation in which all of the premises would be true but the conclusion would be false.

Examples such as these demonstrate that the validity of an inference depends upon its form or structure, not on its content.

Reasoning skills are often assessed through problems involving syllogisms, which are deductive arguments consisting of two premises and a conclusion. Two kinds of syllogisms are particularly common. In a categorical syllogism the premises and the conclusion state that some or all members of one category are or are not members of another category, as in the following examples:

All robins are birds. All birds are animals. Therefore, all robins are animals.

Some bachelors are not astronauts. All bachelors are human beings. Therefore, some human beings are not astronauts.

A linear syllogism involves a quantitative comparison in which each term displays either more of less of a particular attribute or quality, and the reasoner must draw conclusions based on the quantification. An example of a reasoning problem based on a linear syllogism is: "John is taller than Bill, and Bill is taller than Pete. Who is tallest?" Linear syllogisms can also involve negations, as in "Bill is not as tall as John."

INDUCTION

Many aspects of problem solving involve inductive reasoning, or induction. Simply put, induction is a means of reasoning from a part to a whole, from particulars to generals, from the past to the future, or from the observed to the unobserved. Whereas valid deductive inferences guarantee the truth of their conclusions, in the sense that it is impossible for the premises to be true and the conclusion false, good inductive inferences guarantee only that, if the premises are true, the conclusion is probable, or likely to be true. There are several major kinds of inductive reasoning, including causal inference, categorical inference, and analogical inference.

In a causal inference, one reasons to the conclusion that something is, or is likely to be, the cause of something else. For example, from the fact that one hears the sound of piano music, one may infer that someone is (or was) playing a piano. But although this conclusion may be likely, it is not certain, since the sounds could have been produced by an electronic synthesizer.

In a categorical inference, one makes a judgment about whether something is, or is likely to be, a member of a certain category. For example, upon seeing an animal one has never seen before, a person with a limited knowledge of dogs may be confident that what he is seeing is a dog but less certain about the specific species.

In reasoning by analogy, one applies what one has learned to another domain. Aristotle stated the formulae for two possible analogical inferences: "As A is to B, so C is to D"; and "As A is in B, so C is in D." Analogical inference involves applying the outcomes of a known situation to a new or unknown situation. A risk in this approach, however, can occur if the two situations are too dissimilar to merit the analogous comparison.

JUDGMENT

A simple form of realistic thinking—i.e., thinking that is oriented toward the external environment—underlies the ability to discriminate discrete objects or items of information (e.g., distinguishing a lion from a tiger). The outcome is a judgment, and accordingly the process may be called decision making. The availability of information, the rate at which it is presented, the expectations of the person making the judgment, and the number of alternatives available influence the judgment's accuracy and efficiency. Redundancy (or surplus) of information facilitates judgment. For example, a lion may be identified on the basis of a number of different sensory cues, such as being tan or brown, lacking stripes, having a mane, and so on.

CONCEPT ATTAINMENT

A more complex form of realistic thinking underlies the ability to identify or use a class of items, as in selecting several different kinds of triangle from an array of other geometric figures. In the course of solving the problem, the individual will link together a newly experienced group of objects according to one or more of their common properties. This new grouping is then given a general name (as in first learning the meaning of the word *triangle*). It might also be determined that a new object fits an existing category. Physical objects are multidimensional; that is, they may vary in shape, size, colour, location (in relation to other objects), emotional significance, or connotative meaning. How

Artists like this man are among the many groups who employ creative thinking.

a person identifies such dimensions, develops hypotheses (or tentative conclusions) about which of the specific dimensions define a class, arrives at the rules of class membership, and tests various hypotheses all reflect his ability to grasp concepts. Successful performance in all these processes leads to the formulation of pertinent rules based on one's ability to classify specific items.

CREATIVE THINKING

As discussed above, divergent (or creative) thinking is an activity that leads to new information, or previously undiscovered solutions. Some problems demand flexibility, originality, fluency, and inventiveness, especially those for which the individual must supply a unique solution.

A number of processes or phases have been identified as typical of creative thinking. According to one well-known theory, in the first phase—preparation—the thinker assembles and explores resources, perhaps making preliminary decisions about their value in solving the problem at hand. Incubation represents the next phase, in which the individual mulls over possibilities and shifts from one to another relatively freely and without any rigid rational or logical preconceptions and constraints. Illumination occurs when resources fall into place and a definite decision is reached about the result or solution. Next is verification (refinement or polishing), the process of making relatively minor modifications in committing ideas to final form. Often enough, objective standards for judging creative activity (e.g., musical composition) are lacking, especially if the emotional satisfaction of the creator is an important criterion. Although the four phases have been ordered in a logical sequence, they often vary widely and proceed in different orders from one person to the next. Many creative people attain their goals by following special strategies that are not neatly describable.

The phases of preparation, incubation, illumination, and verification are characteristic of creative thinkers generally but do not guarantee that a worthwhile product will ensue. Results also depend on whether an

43

individual has the necessary personality characteristics and abilities; in addition, the quality of creative thinking stems from the training of the creator. The artist who produces oil paintings needs to learn the brushing techniques basic to the task; the scientist who creates a new theory does so against a background of previous learning. Furthermore, creativity intimately blends objective and subjective processes; the successful creator learns how to release and to express his feelings and insights.

Creative thinking is a matter of using intrinsic resources to produce tangible results. This process is markedly influenced by early experience and training. Thus, school and work situations that encourage individual expression and that tolerate idiosyncratic or unorthodox thinking seem to foster the development of creativity.

CHAPTER THREE

MEMORY

Simply put, memory is the encoding, storage, and retrieval of past experiences. The fact that experiences influence subsequent behaviour is evidence of an obvious but nevertheless remarkable activity called remembering. Memory is both a result of and an influence on perception, attention, and learning. The basic pattern of remembering consists of attention to an event followed by the representation of that event in the brain. Repeated attention, or practice, results in a cumulative effect on memory and enables activities such as a skillful performance on a musical instrument, the recitation of a poem, and reading and understanding words on a page. Learning could not occur without the function of memory. So-called intelligent behaviour demands memory, remembering being prerequisite to reasoning. The ability to solve any problem or even to recognize that a problem exists depends on memory. Routine action, such as the decision to cross a street, is based on remembering numerous earlier experiences. The act of remembering an experience and bringing it to consciousness at a later time requires an association, which is formed from the experience, and a "retrieval cue," which elicits the memory of the experience.

Practice (or review) tends to build and maintain memory for a task or for any learned material. During a period without practice, what has been learned tends to be forgotten. Although the adaptive value of forgetting may not be obvious, dramatic instances of sudden forgetting (as in amnesia) can be seen to be adaptive. In this sense, the ability to forget can be interpreted as having been naturally selected in animals. Indeed, when one's memory of an emotionally painful experience leads to severe

Learning can be defined as the alteration of behaviour as a result of individual experience. It is dependent on memory.

anxiety, forgetting may produce relief. Nevertheless, an evolutionary interpretation might make it difficult to understand how the commonly gradual process of forgetting was selected for.

In speculating about the evolution of memory, it is helpful to consider what would happen if memories failed to fade. Forgetting clearly aids orientation in time; since old memories weaken and new ones tend to be vivid, clues are provided for inferring duration. Without forgetting, adaptive ability would suffer; for example, learned behaviour that might have been correct a decade ago may no longer be appropriate or safe. Indeed, cases are recorded of people who (by ordinary standards) forget so little that their everyday activities are full of confusion. Thus, forgetting seems to serve the survival not only of the individual but of the entire human species.

Additional speculation posits a memory-storage system of limited capacity that provides adaptive flexibility specifically through forgetting. According to this view, continual adjustments are made between learning or memory storage (input) and forgetting (output). There is evidence in fact that the rate at which individuals forget is directly related to how much they have learned. Such data offer gross support for models of memory that assume an input-output balance.

Whatever its origins, forgetting has attracted considerable investigative attention. Much of this research has been aimed at discovering those factors that change the rate of forgetting. Efforts are made to study how information may be stored, or encoded in the human brain. Remembered experiences may be said to consist of encoded collections of interacting information, and interaction seems to be a prime factor in forgetting.

Memory researchers have generally supposed that anything that influences the behaviour of an organism endowed with a central nervous system leaves—somewhere in that system—a "trace" or group of traces. So long as these traces endure, they can, in theory, be restimulated, causing the event or experience that established them to be remembered.

TIME-DEPENDENT ASPECTS OF MEMORY

Research by the American psychologist and philosopher William James (1842–1910) led him to distinguish two types of memory: primary, for handling immediate concerns, and secondary, for managing a storehouse of information accumulated over time. Memory researchers have since used the term *short-term memory* to refer to the primary or short-lived memory functions identified by James. Long-term memory refers to the relatively permanent information that is stored in and retrieved from the brain.

WORKING MEMORY

Some aspects of memory can be likened to a system for storing and efficiently retrieving information. One system in particular—identified as "working memory" by the British psychologist Alan Baddeley—is essential for problem solving or the execution of complex cognitive tasks. It is characterized by two components: short-term memory and "executive attention." Short-term memory comprises the extremely limited number of items that humans are capable of keeping in mind at one time, whereas executive attention is a function that regulates the quantity and type of information that is either accepted into or blocked from short-term memory. Baddeley likened working memory to a scratch pad in which essential pieces of information are inscribed and later discarded (or, as is more likely the case, replaced by more pertinent information).

EXECUTIVE ATTENTION

In its role of managing information in short-term memory, executive attention is highly effective in blocking potentially distracting information from the focus of attention. This is one way in which the brain is able to keep information active and in focus. Yet there are limits to the amount of information ("capacity") that executive attention is capable of handling at any given time, and this capacity will differ from person to person. As a result, all people differ in their ability to bring attention to bear on the control of thought. Known as "working memory capacity," this ability is measured most often through a test that requires people to commit a short list of items to memory while performing some other task. Thus, one form of the test might involve reading a series of sentences and then attempting to recall the letters at

Short-term memory makes it possible for people to understand long, complex sentences.

the end of each sentence. The capacity of working memory is measured by the number of items that a person recalls, so that if a person recalls five letters, the working memory capacity in this case is five. In most cases number of letters recalled will depend on each person's ability to avoid the distraction of reading the sentences. Such tests of working-memory capacity can be used to predict an individual's ability to perform tasks involved in reasoning. In fact, working memory capacity is strongly related to general intelligence.

In terms of brain activity, executive attention seems to involve the frontal lobes. Thus, damage to the frontal lobes, which is associated with a condition called dysexecutive syndrome, can affect the role of executive attention in the control of thought, behaviour, and emotion. Evidenced by a notable reduction in the patient's abilities to set goals, make plans, and initiate actions, dysexecutive syndrome is often accompanied by diminished social inhibitions and thereby leads to behaviour that is considered rude or inappropriate. Excessive use of alcohol and other drugs can lead to similar behavioral problems.

PATTERNS OF ACQUISITION IN WORKING MEMORY

In the course of a typical day, humans receive a continuous stream of information from the world around them as well as from their own thought processes and physical experiences. They manage this constant stimulation through a combination of conscious and unconscious effort. The majority of the information is processed (or ignored) unconsciously, because the brain is incapable of consciously attending to and filtering every bit of stimulation it receives. Other forms of information that are processed through unconscious effort, such as a loud sound or a sudden bright light, tend to capture attention in various ways. While events that elicit such attention are more likely to be remembered, especially if they need to be retrieved for possible use in the future, the more significant processes of conscious attention are volitional, occurring in everyday actions such as driving, reading a book, playing chess, watching a basketball game, and following a recipe in a cookbook. The level of attention given to an experience, and the way a person thinks about it, will influence how well the memory for the event is acquired and how well it will be recalled. Researchers also have determined that the techniques employed by the brain in acquiring information differ depending on whether the information is intended for short-term or long-term use.

Most people are capable of storing a maximum of about seven separate units of information in short-term memory—e.g., the seven random letters F, L, I, X, T, Z, R. Thus, one may consult a directory for a 10-digit telephone number but forget some of the digits before one has finished dialing. However, if the units of information are grouped or "chunked" into meaningful patterns, it is possible to recall many more of them, as shown by the series of 24 letters F, R, A, N, C, E, G, E, R, M, A, N, Y, P, O, L, A, N, D, S, P, A, I, N. According to the American psychologist George A. Miller, such chunking of information is essential for short-term memory and plays an important role in learning.

Short-term memory is restricted in both capacity and duration: a limited amount of information will remain active for a few seconds at best unless renewed attention to the information successfully reactivates it in working memory. Before such "renewal" occurs, most information arrives in working memory through sensory inputs, the two most prevalent being aural and visual. Baddeley posited that working memory is supported by two systems: the phonological loop, which processes aural information, and the visuospatial sketch pad, which processes visual and spatial information. When information is acquired aurally, the brain encodes the information according to the way it sounds. A person who hears a spoken telephone number and retains the information long enough to complete dialing is employing the phonological loop, a function of working memory involving, in effect, an inner voice and inner ear each person utilizes to rehearse and recall information. Children who are slow to learn this type of encoding are also generally delayed in learning to read.

Visual and spatial encoding are an integral part of daily problem solving. A person solves a jigsaw puzzle by constructing an image of a missing piece and then seeking the piece that matches the constructed image. It would not make sense for this construct to be held in long-term memory, but its function as a short-term memory is essential to reaching a solution. Such short-term encoding of visual-spatial information is important in any number of tasks, such as packing suitcases in the trunk of a car or searching for a missing shoe in the bottom of a closet.

51

LONG-TERM MEMORY

Memories that endure outside of immediate consciousness are known as "long-term" memories. They may be about something that happened many years ago, such as who attended one's fifth birthday party, or they may concern relatively recent experiences, such as the courses that were served at a luncheon earlier in the day.

Accumulated evidence suggests that a long-term memory is a collection of information augmented by retrieval attributes that allow a person to distinguish one particular memory from all of the other memories stored in the brain. The items stored in long-term memory represent facts as well as impressions of people, objects, and actions. They can be classified as either "declarative" or "nondeclarative," depending on whether their content is such that it can be expressed by a declarative sentence. Thus, declarative memories, like declarative sentences, contain information about facts and events. Nondeclarative memory, also known as procedural memory, is the repository of information about basic skills, motor (muscular) movement, verbal qualities, visual images, and emotions. A crosscutting distinction is made between memories that are tied to a particular place and time, known as "episodic" memories, and those that lack such an association, known as "semantic" memories. The latter category includes definitions and many kinds of factual knowledge, such as knowledge of the name of the current pope, which one might not recall having learned at any particular time or place.

PATTERNS OF ACQUISITION IN LONG-TERM MEMORY

There are roughly three phases in the life of a long-term memory. It must be acquired or learned; it must be stored or retained over time; and, if it is to be of any value, it must be successfully retrieved. These three phases are known as acquisition, storage, and retrieval. Relatively little is known about the factors influencing the storage of memory over time, but a good deal is understood about the mechanisms by which memories are acquired and successfully retrieved.

Memory researchers have identified specific techniques for improving one's ability to remember information over a long period of time. One of the most powerful means involves scheduling regular practice sessions over a relatively long period. Consider, for example, two groups of people learning vocabulary words in a foreign language. One group studies for five hours on one day, and the other group studies for one hour per day for five days in a row. Although both groups practice for a total of five hours, they will differ in their ability to recall what they have learned. If the two groups are tested on the day after the first group studied for five hours, the first group will perform better than the second. If, on the other hand, the test occurs one week after the two groups completed their study, the second group will perform better and remember more of the words in the future. Such cases suggest that, while there may be some short-term benefit to "cramming" for a test, the most effective means of committing facts to long-term memory depends upon routine and repetitive study.

Although the ability to commit information to memory is greatly enhanced through repetition or rehearsal, not all rehearsal techniques are effective in facilitating later recall. Simply saying something to oneself over and over again, a technique called "rote rehearsal," helps to retain the information in short-term memory but does little to build a long-term memory of the event. Another form of rehearsal involves motor coordination, whereby movements or series of movements are "memorized" for greater efficiency or skill of execution in the future. A skilled touch typist who frequently inputs a short string of letters might thereby encode the movements involved in typing the full string, rather than relying on the separate movements he has already encoded for each letter. In this sense rehearsal occurs through repeated attention to each of several movements in a series. This form of rehearsal enables the performance of countless activities, such as riding a bicycle, dancing a particular step, or executing a competitive dive.

More-effective types of rehearsal consist of reflection—thinking about the material one is trying to learn and discovering ways in which it is related to something one already knows. One traditional technique for committing a list of items to memory involves imagining that one is traveling a familiar route in one's town while stopping to place an image of each item at specific landmarks on the route. This technique, called the method of loci, was used by Greek orators such as Cicero and Simonides as a means of organizing and remembering points in their speeches.

The method of loci is based on the principle that encoding new information—such as items from the list to be memorized—to previously stored data—landmarks along a familiar route in one's town—can be an effective means of improving memory function. When encoding techniques are formally applied, they are called mnemonic systems or devices. (The popular rhyme that begins "Thirty days hath September" is an example.) Verbal learning can be enhanced by an appropriate mnemonic system. Thus, paired associates (e.g., DOG-CHAIR) will be learned more rapidly if they are included in a simple sentence (e.g., The dog jumped over the chair). Imagery that can associate different words to be learned (even in a bizarre fashion) has been found beneficial. Indeed, some investigators hold that pure rote learning (in which no use is made of established memories except to directly perceive the stimuli) is rare or nonexistent. They suggest that all learning elaborates on memories that are already available.

Factors that influence the rate of learning should be distinguished from those that affect the rate of forgetting. For example, nonsense syllables are learned more slowly than are an equal number of common words; if both are studied for the same length of time, the better-learned common words will be forgotten more slowly. But this does not mean that the rate of forgetting intrinsically differs for the two tasks. Degree of learning must be held constant before it may be judged whether there are differences in rate of forgetting; rates of

Acronyms can be mnemonic devices. For example, ROYGBIV lists the sequence of colors that make up a rainbow.

forgetting can be compared only if tasks are learned to an equivalent degree. Indeed, when degree of learning is experimentally controlled, different kinds of information are forgotten at about the same rate. Nonsense syllables are not forgotten more rapidly than are ordinary words. In general, factors that seem to produce wide differences in rate of learning show little (if any) effect on rate of forgetting, though some studies of mnemonic systems have demonstrated that pictorial (visual) mnemonics are associated with longer-held memories.

PHYSIOLOGICAL ASPECTS OF LONG-TERM MEMORY

Investigators concerned with the physiological bases of memory seek a kind of neurochemical code with enough physical stability to produce a structural change or memory trace (engram) in the nervous system; mechanisms for decoding and retrieval also are sought. Efforts at the strict behavioral level similarly are directed toward describing encoding, decoding, and retrieval mechanisms as well as the content of the stored information.

One way to characterize a memory (or memory trace) is to identify the information it encodes. A learner may encode far more information than is apparent in the task as presented. For example, if a subject is shown three words for a few seconds and, after 30 seconds of diversion or distraction, is asked to repeat the process of learning-delay-recall with three new word groups, poorer and poorer recall will be observed on successive trials in cases where all of the word groups share some common element (e.g., all are animal names). Such findings may be explained by assuming that the learner encodes this animal category as part of his memory for each word. Initially, the common category might be expected to aid recall by sharply delimiting the number of probable words. Successive triads, however, tend to be encoded in increasingly similar ways, blurring their unique characteristics for the subject. An additional step provides critical supporting evidence for such an interpretation. If a final triad of vegetable names is unexpectedly presented, recall recovers dramatically. The person being tested will tend to reproduce the vegetable names much better than he does those of the last animal triad, and recall will be roughly as efficient as it was for the first three animal names. This shift in word category seems to provide escape from earlier confusion or blurring, and it may be inferred that a common conceptual characteristic was encoded for each animal name.

Any characteristic or attribute of a word may be investigated in this way to determine whether it is incorporated in memory. When recall does not recover, it may be inferred that the manipulated characteristic has little or no representation in memory. For example, grammatical class typically does not appear to be encoded; decrement in recall produced after a series of triads consisting of verbs tends to continue when a shift is made to adjectives. Such an experiment does not indicate what common encoding characteristic might be responsible for the decrement, suggesting only that it is not grammatical class.

Encoding mechanisms also may be inferred from tests of recognition. In one kind of experiment, for example, subjects study a long list of words, being informed of a multiple-choice memory test to follow. Each word is made part of a test question that includes other carefully chosen new words, or "distractors." Distractors are selected to represent the different types of encoding the investigator suspects may have occurred in learning. If the word selected for study is chosen by the subject, little can be inferred about the nature of the encoding. Any errors, however, can be most suggestive. Thus, if the word to be studied was TABLE, the multiple-choice list of words might be TABLE, CHAIR, ABLE, FURNITURE, PENCIL, with TABLE being the only correct answer. If CHAIR is incorrectly selected, it may be suspected that this associatively related word occurred to the subject implicitly during learning and became so well encoded that the subject later could not determine whether it or TABLE had been presented for memorization. If the wrong choice is ABLE, acoustical resemblance to TABLE may have contributed to the confusion. If FURNITURE is erroneously chosen, it is likely that the conceptual category was prominent in the encoding. Finally, because it is not related in any obvious way to TABLE, the word PENCIL may be intended as a control, unlikely to be a part of the memory for TABLE. If this is the case, subjects will be more likely to select distractor words such as PENCIL (or any others that have been encoded along with TABLE).

It is important to note the limitations on what may be inferred from experiments of this kind. Although a subject may have encoded in ways suggested by particular distractors, he still may be able to choose the correct word. Or, even if he chooses one of the distractor words, he still may have encoded in ways not represented by that word.

RETRIEVAL

The common experience of having a name or word on the tip of the tongue seems related to specific perceptual (e.g., visual or auditory) attributes. In particular, people who report a "tip-of-the-tongue" experience usually are able to identify the word's first letter and the number of syllables with an accuracy that far exceeds mere guessing. There is evidence that memories may encode information about when they were established and about how often they have been experienced. Some seem to embrace spatial information; e.g., one remembers a particular news item to be on the lower right-hand side of the front page of a newspaper. Research indicates that the rate of forgetting varies for different attributes. For example, memories in which auditory attributes seem dominant tend to be more rapidly forgotten than those with minimal acoustic characteristics.

The Canadian psychologist Endel Tulving has demonstrated that, while information may be retained over a long period of time, there is no guarantee it will be retrieved precisely when it is needed. Successful retrieval is much more likely if a person is tested in a physical setting (context) that is naturally associated with the event or fact. In cases where the context during the recall test differs from the setting in which the learning occurred, retrieval will be less likely. This is why the name of a colleague from school or work may be difficult to recall if one happens to encounter her at a shopping mall. In such cases, the new setting interferes with one's ability to retrieve the person's name from long-term memory.

Memory can be aided by any number of cues, however. It would be far easier to recall the colleague's name if one were asked to choose it from a list. In general, "recognition memory" (involved in choosing the correct answer from a list) is more reliable than recall memory (retrieving information without any clue or hint that could assist in the retrieval). For this reason most students prefer multiple-choice tests to essay tests.

If a designated (target) memory consists of a collection of attributes, its recall or retrieval should be enhanced by any cue that represents or suggests one of the attributes. A person who fails to recall the word *horse*, for example, may suddenly remember it when he is told that there was an animal name on the list of words he studied. Or he may remember it when presented with an associated term such as *barn* or *zebra*. While recall can be enhanced somewhat by cues, failures are common even with cues that are highly relevant. In sum, if words were not encoded or stored in the brain with accompanying attributes at the time of learning, cuing of any kind would be ineffective.

Retrieval is also influenced by the way in which information is organized in memory. Although it is possible to name all of the Canadian provinces and territories by randomly recalling the names that come to mind, a far more reliable means would be to recall the information systematically, say by geographic region or by alphabetical order.

The passage of time is another phenomenon that influences the successful recall of stored information. If a person is asked to name the opponents his favourite basketball team played last season and the score of each game, his responses usually will be most accurate for the games played at the beginning and the end of the season. Similarly, a person asked to describe each day of an extended journey will best retrieve his memory of events that occurred during the beginning and the end of the trip. In a similar test, a person who is asked to recall the words on a list she has just viewed will recall the initial words in the list best ("primacy effects") and those at the end next best ("recency effects"), while items from the middle are least likely to be recalled. This outcome will be consistent as long as recall begins immediately following presentation of the last word. If, however, a short interval follows that prevents the subject from rehearsing the contents of the list, the recency effect may disappear completely, causing words at the end of the list to be recalled no better than those appearing in the middle. Thus, while primacy effects remain essentially undisturbed, a delay as short as 15 seconds can abolish the recency phenomenon. Although some researchers have suggested that recency effects depend on a separate short-term memory system while primacy effects are mediated by a long-term system, it is possible that a single memory function influences these outcomes.

RELEARNING

The number of successive trials a subject takes to reach a specified level of proficiency may be compared with the number of trials he later needs to attain the same level. This yields a measure of retention by what is called the relearning method. The fewer trials needed to reach the original level of mastery, the better the subject seems to remember. The relearning measure sometimes is expressed as a so-called savings score. If 10 trials initially were required, and 5 relearning trials later produce the same level of proficiency, then 5 trials have been saved; the savings score is 50 percent (that is, 50 percent of the original 10 trials). The more forgetting, the lower the savings score.

Although it may seem paradoxical, relearning methods can yield both sensitive and insensitive measures of forgetting. Tasks have been devised that produce wide differences in recall but for which no differences in relearning are observed. (Some theorists attribute this to a form of heavy interference among learned data that has only momentary influence on retention.) Six months or a year after initial learning, some tests may give zero recall scores but can show savings in relearning. This suggests a cumulative effect, whereby previously acquired knowledge enhances future learning.

AUTOBIOGRAPHICAL MEMORY

As an aspect of episodic memory, autobiographical memories are unique to each individual. The study of autobiographical memory poses problems, because it is difficult to prove whether the events took place as reported. Using diary methods, researchers have found that people recall actions more accurately than thoughts—except in the case of

FALSE MEMORY SYNDROME

Also called recovered memory, pseudomemory, and memory distortion, the false memory experience, usually found in the context of adult psychotherapy, consists of seeming to remember events that never actually occurred. These pseudomemories are often quite vivid and emotionally charged, especially those representing acts of abuse or violence committed against the subject during childhood.

It is not entirely clear how pseudomemories come about, but certain therapeutic practices are considered likely to reinforce and encourage their creation. For example, some therapists use hypnosis or techniques of "guided imagery" on patients who appear to be suffering from the suppression of memories of emotionally disturbing events, often experienced during childhood. Encouraged to visualize episodes of violence or abuse during therapy, patients may subsequently have difficulty separating these imaginary events from reality. Researchers have found that people who "recover" pseudomemories of trauma are often more suggestible and more prone to dissociate—that is, to feel separated from their actual experiences—than most other people.

Questions about the authenticity of memories recovered in therapy have led to debate between various academic, legal, and medical professionals. Because the patient's purported memories often concern events that allegedly occurred many years in the past and in private, they are often difficult or impossible to corroborate.

In response to controversies that emerged in the mid-1990s surrounding recovered memory and reports of abuse, in 1995 the American Psychological Association (APA) recommended

Continued on page 62

Continued from page 61

that those seeking psychotherapy be cautious of therapists who instantly accept or dismiss explanations of childhood abuse. The organization further stated that childhood abuse is not correlated with any specific set of symptoms in adulthood.

emotionally charged thoughts, which are particularly well remembered. Although very few errors are made by those undergoing tests of autobiographical memory, any errors typically involve mixing the details of separate events into one episode. Another method for testing autobiographical memory involves asking subjects to associate particular autobiographical memories with various cue words, such as *window* or *rain*.

EYEWITNESS MEMORY

Conflicting accounts by eyewitnesses demonstrate that memory is not a perfect recording of events from the past; indeed, it is actually a reconstruction of past events. A particularly striking demonstration of the inaccuracy of eyewitness testimony comes from dozens of cases in which those convicted of serious crimes were freed from prison because DNA evidence proved they were not guilty. In most of these cases, the individuals had been convicted on the basis of eyewitness testimony.

Many phenomena can degrade the accuracy of memories. For example, the memory of an eyewitness to a crime may be distorted if she reads news accounts of the crime

that contain photographs of a person suspected of committing it. Later, the eyewitness may erroneously believe that the suspect in the news account is the person whom she saw commit the crime. In this case, memory of the crime and memory of the photograph blend to create a vivid—albeit incorrect—memory of an event that never occurred. Such inaccuracies are not uncommon. The American psychologist Elizabeth Loftus showed that even the manner in which people are questioned about an event can alter their memory of it. Other studies have shown that psychotherapists may inadvertently implant false memories in the

Different eye witnesses will often recall the same scene differently.

minds of their clients. Such outcomes illustrate the degree to which imagination can have powerful effects on memory.

False memories also can be created in laboratory experiments. Subjects who are asked to study a list of words that are related to a particular nonpresented word will claim to remember seeing the nonpresented word. For example, after studying the words *bed*, *rest*, *wake*, *tired*, *awake*, *dream*, *doze*, *blanket*, *snooze*, *drowsy*, *snore*, and *nap*, a large number of subjects will claim to recall seeing the word *sleep*, even though it was not on the list. Although false memories created in laboratory settings differ from false memories of real-world events, they cast light on the processes involved in the creation and maintenance of memory errors, as demonstrated in research by the American psychologists Henry Roediger and Kathleen McDermott.

FORGETTING

When a memory of a past experience is not activated for days or months, forgetting tends to occur. Yet it is erroneous to think that memories simply fade over time. The steps involved are, in fact, far more complex. In seeking to understand forgetting in the context of memory, such auxiliary phenomena as differences in the rates of forgetting for different kinds of information also need to be be taken into account.

It has been suggested that, as time passes, the physiological bases of memory tend to change. With disuse, according to this view, the neural engram (the memory trace in the brain) gradually decays or loses its clarity. While such a theory seems reasonable, it would, if left at this point, do little more than restate behavioral evidence of forgetting at the nervous-system level. Decay or deterioration does not seem attributable merely to the passage of time; some underlying physical process needs to be demonstrated. Until a neurochemical basis for memory can be more explicitly described, any decay theory of forgetting must await detailed development.

INTERFERENCE

A prominent theory of forgetting at the behavioral level is anchored in the phenomenon of interference, or inhibition, which can be either retroactive or proactive. In retroactive inhibition, new learning interferes with the retention of old memories; in proactive inhibition, old memories interfere with the retention of new learning. Both phenomena have great implications for all kinds of human learning.

In a typical study of interference, subjects are asked to learn two successive verbal lists. The following day some are asked to recall the first list and others to recall the second. A third (control) group learns only one list and is asked to recall it a day later. People who learn two lists nearly always recall fewer words than those in the control group.

Theorists attribute the loss produced by these procedures to interference between list-learning tasks. When lists are constructed to exhibit varying differences, the degree of interference seems to be related to the amount of similarity. Thus, loss in recall will be reduced when two successive lists have no identical terms. Maximum loss generally will occur when there appears to be heavy (but not complete) overlap in the memory attributes for the two lists. One may recall parts of the first list in trying to remember the second and vice versa. (This breakdown in discrimination may reflect the presence of dominant attributes that are appropriate for items in both lists.) Discrimination tends to deteriorate as the number of lists increases, retroactive and proactive inhibition increasing correspondingly, suggesting interference at the time of recall.

In retroactive inhibition, however, not all of the loss need be attributed to competition at the moment of recall. Some of the first list may be lost to memory in learning the second; this is called unlearning. If one is asked to recall from both lists combined, first-list items are less likely to be remembered than if the second list had not been learned. Learning the second list seems to act backward in time (retroactively) to destroy some memory of the first. Much effort has been devoted to studying the conditions that affect unlearning, which has become a major topic in interference theory.

Retroactive and proactive effects can be quite gross quantitatively. If one learns a list one day and tries to recall it the next, learns a second list and attempts recall for it the following day, learns a third, and so on, recall for each successive list tends to decline. Roughly 80 percent recall may be anticipated for the first list; this declines steeply to about 20 percent for the 10th list. Learning the earlier lists seems to act forward in time (proactively) to inhibit retention of later lists. These proactive phenomena indicate that the more one learns, the more rapidly one forgets. Similar effects can be demonstrated for retroactive inhibition within just one laboratory session.

Such powerful effects have led some researchers to speculate that all forgetting is produced by interference. Any given memory is said to be subject to interference from others established earlier or subsequently. Interference, theoretically, may occur when memories conflict through any attributes. With a limited group of attributes and an enormous number of memories, it might seem that ordinary attempts at recall would be chaotic. Yet even if all of the memories shared some information, other attributes not held in common could still serve to distinguish them. For example, every memory theoretically is encoded at a different time, and temporal attributes might serve to discriminate otherwise conflicting memories. Indeed, when two apparently conflicting lists are learned several days apart, proactive inhibition is markedly reduced. Assuming that memories are multiply encoded, interference theory need not predict utter confusion in remembering.

Sources of interference are quite pervasive and should not be considered narrowly. For example, all memories seem to be established in specific surroundings or contexts, and subsequent efforts to remember tend to be less effective when the circumstances differ from the original. Alcoholics, when sober, tend to have trouble finding bottles they have hidden while intoxicated; when they drink again, the task is much easier. Some contexts also may be associated with other memories that interfere with whatever it is that one is trying to remember.

Each new memory tends to amalgamate information already in long-term storage. Encoding mechanisms invariably adapt or associate fresh data to information already present, to such an extent that what is encoded may not be a direct representation of incoming stimuli. This is particularly apparent when the input is relatively meaningless; the newly encoded memory comes to resemble those previously established (i.e., it accrues meaning). For example, a nonsense word such as LAJOR might be encoded as MAJOR.

CHALLENGES TO INTERFERENCE THEORY

Although interference theory has attracted wide support as an account of forgetting, it must be placed in perspective. Interpretations that emphasize distinctions between short- and long-term memory and that posit control processes for handling information are potentially more comprehensive than interference theory, and the behavioral evidence for interference eventually may be explained within such systems.

In addition, a number of predictions derived from interference theory have not been well supported by experiment. The focus of difficulty lies in the hypothesis that interference from established memories is a major source of proactive inhibition. The laboratory subject is asked to learn tasks with attributes that have varying degrees of conflict with memories established in daily life. Theoretically, the more conflict, the greater the proactive interference to produce forgetting. Yet a number of experiments have failed to provide much support for this prediction.

Interference theory also fails to account for some pathological forms of forgetting. Repression as observed in psychiatric practice, for example, represents almost complete, highly selective forgetting, far beyond that anticipated by interference theorists. Attempts to study repression through laboratory procedures have failed to yield systematic data that could be used to test theoretical conclusions.

AMNESIA

If humans forgot everything, the consequences would be devastating to their daily lives. It would be impossible to do one's job—much less find one's way to work. Individuals who suffer damage to certain brain regions, particularly the hippocampus, experience this kind of significant memory loss, amnesia, which is marked by an inability to create new long-term memories. In addition, some amnesiacs lose their ability to recall events that occurred before the brain injury, a condition known as retrograde amnesia. Some amnesiacs do not experience deficits in short-term memory, and in many cases their memory deficits appear to be limited to the acquisition and recollection of new associations. If an amnesiac is introduced to a new acquaintance who leaves the room and returns a few minutes later, the amnesic will not remember having met that person. However, amnesiacs are able to remember some types of new information, though they may be unaware that they are remembering. This was proved in the early 20th century by the Swiss psychologist Édouard Claparède, who used a pin to prick an amnesic woman each time he shook her hand. Later the patient would not shake hands with Claparède, even though she could not readily explain why. In her case procedural memory effectively helped her avoid the physical pain that accompanied every act of shaking hands with the physician. Such studies demonstrate that procedural memory can function independently of conscious awareness.

Another form of forgetting is associated with the earliest stages of human development: nearly all people lack the ability to retain memories of experiences they had before they were three years old. Known as infantile amnesia, this universal phenomenon implies that the brain systems required to encode and retrieve specific events are not adequately developed to support long-term memory before age three. Another theory points to developmental changes in the means by which memories are formed and retrieved after early childhood, suggesting that the more-developed brain lacks the ability to access such early memories. Sigmund Freud, in contrast, proposed that infantile amnesia was a form of repression—in other words, a defense mechanism against disagreeable or negative recollections.

Researchers have concluded that the infant brain loses memories far more quickly than does the developed brain and that it lacks the ability to generalize to new events. Children under the age of five or six do not yet realize that learning is most effective when new information is associated meaningfully with other knowledge. Young children are similarly unaware that the intentional rehearsal or repetition of new information will enhance their ability to retain it in memory. As children age and develop language expertise, however, they begin to draw upon their semantic memory to help them remember words, facts, and events. They also grow increasingly aware of the ways in which memory serves them. This awareness of how memory works, known as "metamemory," increases through much of adulthood.

AGING

Older adults experience memory loss, but only for memories of certain types. Episodic memory (the ability to remember specific events) is typically the first type of memory to decline in old age; it is also the last to fully develop in children. Associative memory (the ability to learn, store, and retrieve associations between actions or things) also declines dramatically. In fact, a chief memory complaint among older adults is a decreasing ability to associate a person's name with his face. Studies conducted separately by American psychologists Marcia K. Johnson and Larry L. Jacoby demonstrated that, whereas older adults are able to remember the gist of an action or event just as well as younger adults, they are unable to recollect the specific details that were involved. Older adults also have particular difficulty remembering the source of their memories, even in cases in which the information is familiar. Yet other types of memory are spared in old age—the most common among these being recognition. It is therefore common

Memory loss is a part of aging, but not all types of memory are affected to the same degree.

for an older adult to recognize a person's face while failing to recall that person's name. Jacoby's work measured age-dependent distinctions between familiarity (recognition) and source memory (recollection) of a given event. His studies provided stronger confirmation that recognition abilities are similar in younger and older individuals, but as people age, they are less able to recall specific details of the events related to the familiar person or thing.

Age-related memory deficiencies can stem from a number of causes. Research in the 1990s by the American psychologist Timothy A. Salthouse suggested that age-related declines in working memory, and in the speed by which information is processed, can reduce a person's ability to remember specific details of previous events. Changes in the brains of older adults, especially in the frontal lobes and hippocampal area, also may result in age-related memory deficits. More severe and widespread changes in the brain are related to the massive declines in memory functioning seen in Alzheimer disease, also known as senile dementia of Alzheimer type or SDAT.

CHAPTER FOUR

PERSONALITY

A person's characteristic way of thinking, feeling, and behaving is his or her personality. Personality embraces moods, attitudes, and opinions and is most clearly expressed in interactions with other people. It includes behavioral characteristics, both inherent and acquired, that distinguish one person from another and that can be observed in people's relations to the environment and to the social group.

The intellectual, emotional, and behavioral characteristics of a person make up that person's personality.

The term *personality* has been defined in many ways, but as a psychological concept two main meanings have evolved. The first pertains to the consistent differences that exist between people: in this sense, the study of personality focuses on classifying and explaining relatively stable human psychological characteristics. The second meaning emphasizes those qualities that make all people alike and that distinguish psychological man from other species; it directs the personality theorist to search for those regularities among all people that define the nature of humanity as well as the factors that influence the course of lives. This duality may help explain the two directions that personality studies have taken: on the one hand, the study of ever more specific qualities in people, and, on the other, the search for the organized totality of psychological functions that emphasizes the interplay between organic and psychological events within people and those social and biological events that surround them. The dual definition of personality is interwoven in most of the topics discussed below. It should be emphasized, however, that no definition of personality has found universal acceptance within the field.

The study of personality can be said to have its origins in the fundamental idea that people are distinguished by their characteristic individual patterns of behaviour—the distinctive ways in which they walk, talk, furnish their living quarters, or express their urges. Whatever the behaviour, personologists—as those who systematically study personality are called—examine how people differ in the ways they express themselves and attempt to determine the causes of these differences. Although other fields of psychology examine many of the same functions and processes, such as attention, thinking, or motivation, the personologist places emphasis on how these different processes fit together and become integrated so as to give each person a distinctive identity, or personality. The systematic psychological study of personality has emerged from a number of different sources, including psychiatric case studies that focused on lives in distress, from philosophy, which explores the nature of humanity, and from physiology, anthropology, and social psychology.

In general, information about human personality has come from three different sources of study. The first is that of the biological, or genetic, origins of personality. The second is that of the social realm, including the impact of social forces on the growing child that shape such personal responses as motives, traits, behaviours, and attitudes. The third is the examination of clinical contacts with people who have suffered adaptive and adjustive failures. Some authorities have suggested that a greater degree of integration of all three sources of information and the methods derived from them would accelerate the growth of valid information about personality.

The systematic study of personality as a recognizable and separate discipline within psychology may be said to have begun in the 1930s with the publication in the United States of two textbooks, *Psychology of Personality* (1937) by Ross Stagner and *Personality: A Psychological Interpretation* (1937) by Gordon W. Allport, followed by Henry A. Murray's *Explorations in Personality* (1938), which contained a set of experimental and clinical studies, and by Gardner Murphy's integrative and comprehensive text, *Personality: A Biosocial Approach to Origins and Structure* (1947). Yet personology can trace its ancestry to the ancient Greeks, who proposed a kind of biochemical theory of personality.

PHYSIOLOGICAL TYPE THEORIES

The idea that people fall into certain personality type categories in relation to bodily characteristics has intrigued numerous modern psychologists as well as their counterparts among the ancients. The idea that people must fall into one or another rigid personality class, however, has been largely dismissed. Two general sets of theories are considered here, the humoral and the morphological.

HUMORAL THEORIES

Perhaps the oldest personality theory known is contained in the cosmological writings of the Greek philosopher and physiologist Empedocles and in related speculations of the physician Hippocrates. Empedocles' cosmic elements—air (with its associated qualities, warm and moist), earth (cold and dry), fire (warm and dry), and water (cold and moist)— were related to health and corresponded (in the above order) to Hippocrates' physical humours, which were associated with variations in temperament: blood (sanguine temperament), black bile (melancholic), yellow bile (choleric), and phlegm (phlegmatic). This theory, with its view that body chemistry determines temperament, has survived in some form for more than 2,500 years. According to these early theorists, emotional stability as well as general health depend on an appropriate balance among the four bodily humours; an excess of one may produce a particular bodily illness or an exaggerated personality trait. Thus, a person with an excess of blood would be expected to have a sanguine temperament—that is, to be optimistic, enthusiastic, and excitable. Too much black bile (dark blood perhaps mixed with other secretions) was believed to produce a melancholic temperament. An oversupply of yellow bile (secreted by the liver) would result in anger, irritability, and a "jaundiced" view of life. An abundance of phlegm (secreted in the respiratory passages) was alleged to make people stolid, apathetic, and undemonstrative. As biological science has progressed, these primitive ideas about body chemistry have been replaced by more complex ideas and by contemporary studies of hormones, neurotransmitters, and substances produced within the central nervous system, such as endorphins.

MORPHOLOGICAL THEORIES

Related to the biochemical theories are those that distinguish types of personalities on the basis of body shape (somatotype). Such a morphological (body type) theory was developed by the German psychiatrist Ernst Kretschmer. In his book *Physique and Character*, first published in 1921, he wrote that among his patients a frail, rather weak (asthenic) body build as well as a muscular (athletic) physique were frequently characteristic of schizophrenic patients, while a short, rotund (pyknic) build was often found among manic-depressive patients. Kretschmer extended his findings and assertions in a theory that related body build and personality in all people and wrote that slim and delicate physiques are associated with introversion, while those with rounded heavier and shorter bodies tend to be cyclothymic—that is, moody but often extraverted and jovial.

Despite early hopes that body types might be useful in classifying personality characteristics or in identifying psychiatric syndromes, the relations observed by Kretschmer were not found to be strongly supported by empirical studies. In the 1930s more elaborate studies by American psychologist William H. Sheldon developed a system for assigning a three-digit somatotype number to people, each digit with a range from 1 to 7. Each of the three digits applies to one of Sheldon's three components of body build: the first to the soft, round endomorph; the second to the square, muscular mesomorph; and the third to the linear, fine-boned ectomorph. Thus, an extreme endomorph would be 711, an extreme ectomorph 117, and an average person 444. Sheldon then developed a 20-item list of traits that differentiated three separate categories of behaviours or temperaments. The three-digit temperament scale appeared to be significantly related to the somatotype profile, an association that failed to excite personologists.

Also during the 1930s, personality studies began to consider the broader social context in which a person lived. American anthropologist Margaret Mead studied the patterns of cooperation and competition in 13 primitive societies and was able to document wide variations in those behaviours in different societies. In her book *Sex and Temperament in Three Primitive Societies* (1935), she showed that masculinity is not necessarily expressed through aggressiveness and that femininity is not

Margaret Mead was one of the foremost anthropologists of the 20th century.

necessarily expressed through passivity and acquiescence. These demonstrated variations raised questions about the relative roles of biology, learning, and cultural pressures in personality characteristics.

PSYCHOANALYTIC THEORIES

Perhaps the most influential integrative theory of personality is that of psychoanalysis, which was largely promulgated during the first four decades of the 20th century by the Austrian neurologist Sigmund Freud. Although its beginnings were based in studies of psychopathology, psychoanalysis became a more general perspective on normal personality development and functioning.

FREUD

Freud's field of investigation began with case studies of so-called neurotic conditions, which included hysteria, obsessive-compulsive disorders, and phobic conditions. Patients with hysterical symptoms complained of acute shortness of breath, paralyses, and contractures of limbs for which no physical cause could be found. In the course of interviews, Freud and his early coworker and mentor, the Austrian physician Josef Breuer, noted that many of their patients were unsure of how or when their symptoms developed and even seemed indifferent to the enormous inconvenience the symptoms caused them. It was as if the ideas associated with the symptoms were quarantined from the consciousness and lay neglected by normal curiosity. To explain this strange pattern Breuer and Freud made two assumptions. The first was based on the general scientific position of determinism, which was quite prevalent in 19th-century science: although no apparent physical causes could be implicated, these neurotic symptoms were nevertheless caused, or determined, perhaps not by one but by multiple factors, some of which were psychologically motivated. The second assumption entailed unconscious psychological processes; that is, ideas continue to be active, to change, and to influence behaviour even when they are outside of awareness. One source for this assumption was the observation of posthypnotic suggestion, which seemed to imply that past experiences, surviving outside of consciousness as latent memories, could be activated by a signal from the environment and could then influence behaviour even though the hypnotized person was unaware of the reasons for his behaviour.

Breuer and Freud believed that the specific motivation for these neurotic symptoms lay in the patient's desire to obliterate from memory profoundly distressing events that were incompatible with the patient's moral standards and therefore in conflict with them. These events were considered to have been sexual in nature, and further exploration convinced Freud that his patients had had even earlier troublesome sexual experiences—usually seductions—the memories of which had lain dormant until awakened by a more recent sexual encounter. Freud reasoned that the earlier seduction experience imparted to the later one its pathogenic force. Freud at first accepted many of the experiences reported by his young, impressionable patients as actual seductions. He later came to believe that many, though not all, of the narrations were fantasies. Based upon this conviction Freud formulated a theory indicating that personality is shaped by such experiences as well as by other traumatic or frustrating events. He postulated that the fantasies about sexual traumas were expressions of a sexual drive. Thereafter in Freud's therapeutic method, the search for actual sexual trauma was replaced by an exploration of the ways in which patients' sexual inclinations, already present in childhood, were expressed in behaviour. Neurosis and personality in general came to be viewed as outcomes of conflict between sexual motivations and defenses against them, the conflict being rooted in early child development.

PSYCHOSES AND NEUROSES

Psychoses are major mental illnesses that are characterized by severe symptoms such as delusions, hallucinations, disturbances of the thinking process, and defects of judgment and insight. Persons with psychoses exhibit a disturbance or disorganization of thought, emotion, and behaviour so profound that they are often unable to function in everyday life and may be incapacitated or disabled. Such individuals are often unable to realize that their subjective perceptions and feelings do not correlate with objective reality, a phenomenon evinced by persons with psychoses who do not know or will not believe that they are ill despite the distress they feel and their obvious confusion concerning the outside world. Traditionally, the psychoses have been broadly divided into organic and functional psychoses. Organic psychoses were believed to result from a physical defect of or damage to the brain. Functional psychoses were believed to have no physical brain disease evident upon clinical examination. Much recent research suggests that this distinction between organic and functional is probably inaccurate. Most psychoses are now believed to result from some structural or biochemical change in the brain.

Neuroses, or psychoneuroses, are less-serious disorders in which people may experience negative feelings such as anxiety or depression. Their functioning may be significantly impaired, but personality remains relatively intact, the capacity to recognize and objectively evaluate reality is maintained, and they are basically able to function in everyday life. In contrast to people with psychoses, neurotic patients know or can be made to realize that they are ill, and they usually want to get well and return to a normal state. Their chances for recovery are better than those of persons with psychoses. The symptoms of neurosis may sometimes resemble the coping mechanisms used in everyday life by most people, but in neurotics these defensive reactions are inappropriately severe or prolonged in response to an external stress. Anxiety disorders, phobic disorder (exhibited as unrealistic fear or dread), conversion disorder (formerly known as hysteria), obsessive-compulsive disorder, and depressive disorders have been traditionally classified as neuroses.

Freud assumed that his patients were motivated to ward off those fantasies that had an exciting as well as a repelling quality about them. Freud described various psychological devices (defense mechanisms) by which people tried to make the fantasies bearable. For example, in the obsessive-compulsive condition, which refers to persistent unwelcome ideas or recurrent irresistible urges to perform certain acts, such as incessant hand washing, the defense maneuvers are called isolation and displacement. They consist in separating (isolating) a fantasy from its corresponding emotion, and then attaching (displacing) the emotion to another, previously trivial idea; for instance, to the hand washer it is the hands that are dirty rather than the desires. Freud also noted that people who rely on isolation and displacement are otherwise characterized by nonpathological personality qualities such as perfectionism, indecisiveness, and formality in interpersonal contacts. To Freud the fantasies were the mental representations of basic drives, among which sex, aggression, and self-preservation were paramount. These drives, moreover, required taming as the child matured into an adult, and the taming process involved blocking out of consciousness some of the ideas associated with the expression of those drives. Other methods of defense include repression, a kind of withholding of conflicting ideas from recall; projection, the attribution to others of one's own rejected tendencies; and reaction formation, turning into its opposite a tendency rejected in oneself—as in excessive generosity as a defense against avarice. The basic conflict between drives and control processes, which Freud believed to be the basis of several neuroses, was also invoked to explain both dream content and the "psychopathology of everyday life"—the ordinary slips of the tongue (sometimes called Freudian slips) and errors such as forgetting intentions or misplacing objects.

These primary human drives, moreover, were seen to undergo transformations as part of psychological and physical growth. This formulation widened the realm of sexuality beyond reproduction, by proposing that genital activity does not encompass all of sexuality, because sexual activity can be observed long before biological maturity and can occur without leading to reproduction. The theory further proposed that sexual maturation develops in a sequence of stages as parts of the body successively yield sensual pleasure to the child, beginning with the mouth, followed by the anus, and then the genitals. Social demands for inhibition and control of the drives centre about the functions of these zones, and it is from this process of socialization that personality is said to emerge. For example, the extent to which the personality expresses power, responsibility, compliance, and defiance seems to coincide with anal expressions of the sexual drive and is related to the process of obtaining control over anal functions.

The conflict between the drives—conceptualized as a wholly unconscious structure called the id—and the drive control processes—conceptualized as a largely unconscious structure called the ego—results in the creation of a characteristic style for mediating conflicts, which is assumed to be formed prior to adolescence. While learning and experience are recognized as conspicuous factors in the shaping of these behaviours, the theory also gives prominence to possibly inborn differences in the strength of drives and of the control processes.

Among the controlling functions of the ego are identifications and defenses. Children are inclined to behave like the significant adult models in their environment, Freud postulated. These identifications give identity and individuality to the maturing child. Moreover, the process of self-criticism is part of the ego controls (Freud called it the superego) and acts as an internal and often unconscious conscience that influences moral values.

JUNG

The Swiss psychiatrist Carl Gustav Jung, an early adherent of Freud's theories, questioned the degree of emphasis that Freud gave to sexual motivations in personality development. Jung accepted the significant effect of the unconscious processes, but unlike Freud he preferred to emphasize that behaviour is motivated more by abstract, even spiritual, processes than by sexual drives. Jung also focused more on individual differences; in particular he developed a typology of reaction styles, distinguishing between two basic means of modulating basic drives, introversion and extraversion. Introversion was defined as preoccupation with one's inner world at the expense of social interactions and extraversion as a preference for social interplay for living out inner drives (collectively termed libido). The existence of these two types receives empirical support from most studies of traits.

ADLER

The Austrian psychiatrist Alfred Adler, another of Freud's early followers, also disputed the importance of sexual motives. Adler described a coping strategy that he called compensation, which he felt was an important influence on behaviour. In his view people compensated for a behavioral deficiency by exaggerating some other behaviour: a process analogous to organic processes called hypertrophy, in which, for example, if one eye is injured, the other eye may compensate by becoming more acute. In Adler's view, a person with a feeling of inferiority related to a physical or mental inadequacy would also develop compensating behaviours or symptoms. Shortness of stature, for example, could lead to the development of domineering, controlling behaviours. Adler assigned a prominent place to family dynamics in personality development. Children's position in their family—their birth order—was seen as determining significant character traits.

ERIKSON

Freud's emphasis on the developmental unfolding of the sexual, aggressive, and self-preservative motives in personality was modified by the American psychoanalyst Erik H. Erikson, who integrated psychological, social, and biological factors. Erikson's scheme proposed eight stages of the development of drives, which continue past Freud's five stages of childhood (oral, anal, phallic, latency, and genital) and through three stages of adulthood. The stages proceed in leaps according to what is called an epigenetic process. The term *epigenesis*, borrowed from embryology, refers to the predetermined developmental sequence of parts of an organism. Each part has a special time for its emergence and for its progressive integration within the functioning whole. Each phase of emergence depends upon the successful completion of the preceding phase. According to Erikson, environmental forces exercise their greatest effect on development at the earliest stages of growth, because anything that disturbs one stage affects all of the following stages. As if controlled by a biological timetable, each given stage must be superseded by a new one, receding in significance as the new stage assumes dominance. A constant interleaving at critical periods—in which some parts emerge while others are suppressed—must proceed smoothly if personality problems are to be avoided.

The Freudian theory of development with Erikson's modifications provides for a succession of drive-control (inner and environmental) interactions. These can be fit into a schema of polar attitudes that develop in progressive stages of a person's life, creating a conflict at each stage which should be resolved to avoid extremes of personality development. Erikson thus evolved his eight stages of development, which he described as: (1) infancy: trust versus mistrust; (2) early childhood:

autonomy versus shame and doubt; (3) preschool: initiative versus guilt; (4) school age: industry versus inferiority; (5) puberty: identity versus identity confusion; (6) young adulthood: intimacy versus isolation; (7) middle adulthood: generativity versus stagnation; and (8) late adulthood: integrity versus despair.

THE IMPACT OF PSYCHOANALYSIS

There is little doubt that psychoanalysis had a profound influence on personality theory during the 20th century. It turned attention from mere description of types of people to an interest in how people become what they are. Psychoanalytic theory emphasizes that the human organism is constantly, though slowly, changing through perpetual interactions, and that, therefore, the human personality can be conceived of as a locus of change with fragile and indefinite boundaries. It suggests that research should focus not only on studies of traits, attitudes, and motives but also on studies that reflect the psychoanalytic view that personality never ceases to develop and that even the rate of personality modification changes during the course of a life. Although the theory holds that conflict and such basic drives as sex and aggression figure prominently in personality development and functioning, their presence may be neither recognizable nor comprehensible to persons untrained to look for those motives. However, personality characteristics are relatively stable over time and across situations, so that a person remains recognizable despite change. Another feature of psychoanalytic theory is the insistence that personality is affected by both biological and psychosocial forces that operate principally within the family, with the major foundations being laid early in life.

The data on which psychoanalytic theory rests came from the psychoanalysts' consulting rooms, where patients in conflict told their life stories to their analysts. No provision is made in that setting for experimental manipulation, for independent observation, or for testing the generality

Psychoanalytic theories of personality tend to emphasize the formative influence of the family.

of the formulations. As a consequence, although much of the theory has found its way into accepted doctrine, psychoanalysis cannot claim a body of experimentally tested evidence. Nevertheless, psychoanalytic theory provides at least a preliminary framework for much of personality research involving motives and development.

TRAIT THEORIES

Contemporary personality studies are generally empirical and based on experiments. While they are more precise, and thus may be more valid than much of psychoanalytic theory, experiments perforce have a narrower scope than the grand sweep of psychoanalysis. In the 1940s many investigators focused on intensive studies of individual traits and of combinations of traits that seemed to define personality types, such as the "authoritarian personality." Others, like the American psychologists David C. McClelland and John W. Atkinson, studied the characteristic presence of certain needs identified by Murray, such as the need for achievement or affiliation. The method used to measure these needs was to examine the fantasy productions of Murray's Thematic Apperception Test (TAT) and to relate the motive score to other behavioral indexes such as personal history, occupational choice, speed of learning, and persistence of behaviour following failure.

STABILITY OF TRAITS

Traits such as sociability, impulsiveness, meticulousness, truthfulness, and deceit are assumed to be more or less stable over time and across situations. Traits refer not to single instances of a behaviour, such as lying, but to persistent although not unvarying behaviour that, according to some personologists, implies a disposition to respond in a particular, identifiable way. According to American psychologist and educator Gordon W. Allport's 1937 textbook, traits represent structures or habits within a person and are not the construction of observers; they are the product of both genetic predispositions and experience. It can be generally stated that traits are merely names for observed regularities in behaviour, but do not explain them. Nevertheless, the study of how traits arise and are integrated within a person forms a major area of personality studies.

In the English language there are several thousand words representing traits, many of them close in meaning to others (for example, *meticulous, careful, conscientious*). Most of the measurement studies employ self-report (personality) inventories that require people to describe themselves by checking relevant adjectives or answering questions about

Sociability, or being inclinced to seek the company of others, is one of the most-studied personality traits.

typical behaviours that they are conscious of displaying. In some measurements, observers rate the behaviour of others. Psychologists such as Hans J. Eysenck in the United Kingdom and Raymond B. Cattell in the United States have attempted to reduce the list to what they could consider to be the smallest possible number of trait clusters. The statistical technique of factor analysis has been favoured for this task, since it explores the correlations among all of the trait names and identifies clusters of correlations among traits that appear to be independent of (uncorrelated with) each other. Common to almost all the trait systems are variables related to emotional stability, energy level, dominance, and sociability, although different investigators choose different names for these factors. Eysenck, for example, has reduced the trait names to but three higher-order factors—introversion–extraversion, neuroticism, and psychoticism—and has attempted to explore the biological roots of each factor.

DEVIATION FROM TRAIT THEORY

The idea that traits represent relatively stable behaviours has received criticism over the years from psychologists who point out that behavioral consistency across situations and across time is not the rule. For example, in a 1928 study of children's moral development, the American psychologists Hugh Hartshorne and Mark A. May placed 10- to 13-year-old children in situations that gave them the opportunity to lie, steal, or cheat; to spend money on themselves or on other children; and to yield to or resist distractions. The predictive power of personal and educational background was low, and children were not found consistently honest or dishonest, distractible, or altruistic. The most powerful predictor of children's behaviour was what other children around them were doing.

In the 1960s and '70s some psychologists, including Walter Mischel and Albert Bandura in the United States, recalled the Hartshorne and May study and variations of it to support their view that behaviour is controlled not by hypothctical traits but according to the degree of regularity of external stimuli. That is, they believe that personality traits are only consistent if the situation is consistent and that they vary once the situation changes. In their view, behavioral consistency does not reflect stable personality traits. Rather, it is the environment that evokes and shapes the illusion of such traits. This would be in keeping with the view of social learning theorists that personality, like other elements of a person's psychological makeup, is largely a learning phenomenon related to such factors as the imitation of role models. Social learning theory would also contend that personality is more susceptible to change than would trait theory.

Although it has been demonstrated that behaviour is seldom entirely consistent, it also has been shown that it reflects considerable consistency. Even in the Hartshorne and May study some children showed consistently honest or dishonest behaviour, and behavioral consistency was found to increase with age.

Support for personal consistency is bolstered by studies of what has been called the fundamental attribution error. The investigators, most of them social psychologists, report that, in observing the behaviour of others, people exaggerate the role of internal causes and invoke traits as a primary cause (e.g., "John acted the way he did because he is honest"). In assigning cause to their own behaviour, however, people more often cite external causes such as the particular situation. These tendencies are accompanied by another discovered regularity: in seeking sources for their own behaviour, people are likely to favour internal causes (and thus agree with an observer's judgment) when they consider a behaviour to be desirable (e.g., success, as in "I was successful because I am skillful"), and they invoke external, situational causes in judging a behaviour they deem undesirable (e.g., failure, as in "I failed because the test was unfair"). There are, of course, limits to the regularity with which these generalizations hold. Because people tend to know their own characteristics better than observers do, they are generally more aware than observers are of any divergences from their usual behaviour.

Although people may assume the existence of traits in themselves, they do not, in analyzing a specific situation, see themselves as a mere collection of trait names. Consequently, they are not for the most part perplexed by, and often do not recognize, cross-situational inconsistency in their own behaviour. But in observing another person's behaviour, most people attribute high consistency to that person, as if many positive traits could be inferred from the attribution or observation of one positive trait. For example, the American social psychologist Solomon Asch has shown that a physically attractive person will tend to be judged as having many other desirable qualities.

Asch also demonstrated that, in forming impressions of the personal characteristics of others, observers are most influenced by their first impression. The reason first impressions seem to be almost indelible is that they carry an excessive amount of new information, which has a high degree of unpredictability. That is, the more new information contained in an event, the more attention it attracts. Since impressions about a person tend to be integrated into a single characterization, an observer may be jarred by recognizing an undesirable fact about an attractive person and may try either to ignore that fact or to mitigate (rationalize) it. These propensities make up a "common sense psychology," in the words of Fritz Heider, an American psychologist. This "naive" psychology, as he called it, consists of a set of rules that guide most people's impressions of other people and of social situations. These rules are used constantly to interpret one's own and other people's behaviour and to predict behaviour under certain conditions. The psychoanalytic view, however, seriously challenges this common sense psychology. Psychoanalysis has no problem explaining that those who put to death countless people in the Nazi death chambers, for example, could also be devoted parents, whereas common sense psychology would have difficulty with this. For the psychoanalyst, a personality may be integrated, but it is rarely seamless and regular. People generally make two types of errors in judging personality: they impute more personality consistency to others than the actors themselves would allow, and they often ignore the operation of unconscious psychological processes that can explain at least some of the inconsistencies.

Much work on trait structure and impression formation has concerned adjectival words that describe traits, and the fact that these studies have been carried out principally in the United States and western Europe has led some anthropologists, such as the American Robert LeVine, to remark that modern personality trait theory is ethnocentric. For example, the folk-psychological concepts and the trait matrices derived from factor analyses include culture-specific assumptions about personal experiences, such as the distinctions between mind and body, natural and supernatural, and intellect and morality, which do not exist in the folk traditions of many non-Western peoples. Unlike most other cultures, Western thought assumes that a high degree of personal autonomy is desirable and that the most important emotional and personal relations are with a marital partner. For some psychologists these cultural differences point to the need for a less culture-bound approach to personality trait theory.

MODERN TRENDS

Modern approaches to personality studies have focused on sex differences, aggression, genetic aspects of personality, and cognitivie controls (or cognitive styles), among other topics.

SEX DIFFERENCES

Despite the physical differences between males and females the finding of behavioral differences between the sexes is controversial. Behaviours associated with sex roles depend heavily on the social and cultural context, and studies of stereotypic male and female roles are therefore understandably ambiguous. Yet some findings indicate small but consistent differences. While there are no differences in measured IQ, itself regarded as a culture-bound assessment, females do better than males on verbal tasks. Girls generally begin to speak earlier than boys and have fewer language problems in school and in the course of maturation. Males generally exhibit greater skill in understanding spatial relations and in solving problems that involve mathematical reasoning. Beginning at the toddler stage, the activity level of males is generally higher than that of females. A related finding is that boys are more likely to be irritable and aggressive than girls and more often behave like bullies. Men usually outscore women in antisocial personality disorders, which consist of persistent lying, stealing, vandalism,

While some studies of sex differences focus on adults, others explore the differences between girls and boys.

and fighting, although these differences do not appear until after about the age of three. A study by the American anthropologists Beatrice B. Whiting and Carolyn P. Edwards found that males were consistently more aggressive than females in seven cultures, suggesting that there is a predisposition in males to respond aggressively to provocative situations, although how and whether the attacking response occurs depends on the social and cultural setting.

AGGRESSION

Humans are perhaps the only species of animal that does not have an internal inhibition against slaughtering other members of the species. It has been theorized that humans, like other animals, are motivated by an aggressive drive, which has significant survival value, but lack internal inhibitions against killing their fellow humans. Inhibitions, therefore, must be imposed externally by society. Social learning theorists emphasize the decisive effects of situations in triggering and controlling aggression. They account for the poor predictability of aggressive behaviour in humans by noting that the environmental context is generally unpredictable. Yet research has shown that an aggressive act is most likely to be produced by a person with a history of aggressive behaviour.

GENETIC ASPECTS

While social learning theorists emphasize the active shaping of personality by external social influences, experimental evidence has accumulated that genetic factors play a prominent role, if not in the transmission of specific behaviour patterns, then in the readiness of people to respond to environmental pressures in particular ways. In observations of animals, it is commonplace to find in different breeds of dogs wide divergences in behaviour that are attributed to genetic differences: some are friendly, others aggressive; some are timid, others bold (of course there may also be wide variations within a given breed). Among human infants observed in a neonatal nursery, there are also clearly observable differences in activity, passivity, fussiness, cuddliness, and responsiveness. These patterns, which some authorities say may be genetically influenced, shape the ways in which the infant will interact with the environment and can be considered an expression of personality.

In systematic studies of humans, studies of twins and adopted children have been used to try to evaluate environmental and genetic factors as determinants of a number of behaviour patterns. These studies

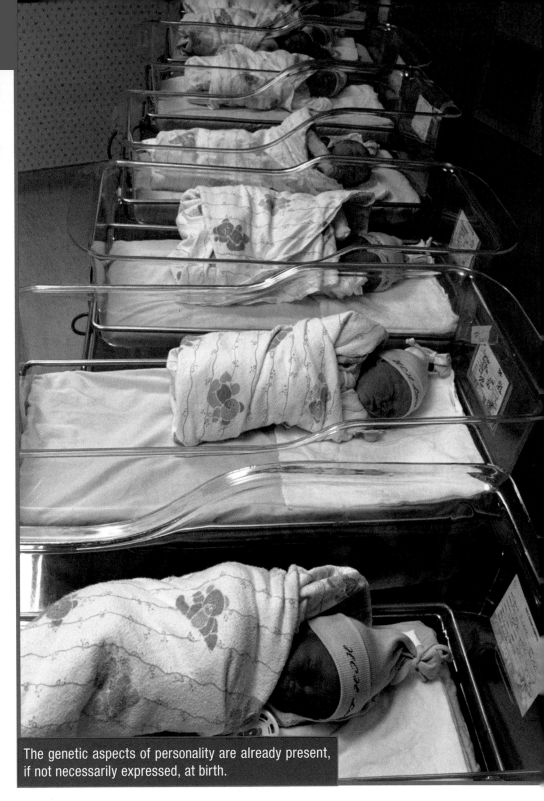

The genetic aspects of personality are already present, if not necessarily expressed, at birth.

have shown that genetic factors account for about 50 percent of the range of differences found in a given population. Most of the remaining differences are attributable not to the environment that is common to members of a family but to the environment that is unique to each member of the family or that results from interactions of family members with one another. In the United States, behaviour geneticists such as Robert Plomin report that, in behaviours describable as sociability, impulsiveness, altruism, aggression, and emotional sensitivity, the similarities among monozygotic (identical) twins is twice that among dizygotic (fraternal) twins, with the common environment contributing practically nothing to the similarities. Similar findings are reported for twins reared together or separately.

The study of the genetic aspects of personality is a relatively new undertaking. Almost all populations studied have been from industrialized Western nations whose rearing environments are more nearly alike than different. It is known that the more homogeneous the environment, the stronger the genetic contribution will appear. As with the psychology of traits, cross-cultural studies are required to test the validity of the claims of behaviour genetics.

COGNITIVE CONTROLS AND STYLES

Psychologists have long been aware that people differ in the consistent way in which they receive and respond to information. Some make careful distinctions between stimuli, whereas others blur distinctions, and some may typically prefer to make broad categories, whereas others prefer narrow ones for grouping objects. These consistencies in an individual seem to be fairly stable across time and even across situations. They have been referred to as cognitive controls. Combinations of several cognitive controls within a person have been referred to as cognitive style, of which there can be numerous variations.

Cognitive control studies explore constraints within a person that limit the influence of both environment and motivation, and as such they are expressions of personality. In the 1940s and '50s several studies explored the extent to which personal needs or drives determine what one perceives. In one study, children from rich and poor families were asked to adjust a circle of light to the size of several coins of increasing value and to the size of cardboard disks. All of the children overestimated the size of the coins, although not of the neutral disks, but the poor children overestimated the sizes more than did the rich children. The assumption that need influences such judgments has been widely held. Even Shakespeare, in *A Midsummer Night's Dream*, noted, "Or in the night, imagining some fear, / how easy is a bush supposed a bear." But there are limits to the distorting power of drives, and the experimental demonstration of the influence of motives has been difficult to confirm, perhaps because the formal components of cognition—the workings, for example, of attention, judgment, or perception—and individual difference in their expression have been neglected by personologists. Investigators of cognitive controls examine the psychological limits on the distorting effects of needs and of external reality. For example, in estimating the size of a disk, some people are more exact than others, and the extent to which a need can distort size judgments will consequently be limited by the perceiver's preference for strict or relaxed standards of comparison.

The American psychologists George S. Klein and Herman Witkin in the 1940s and '50s were able to show that several cognitive controls were relatively stable over a class of situations and intentions. For example, the psychologists found a stable tendency in some people to blur distinctions between successively appearing stimuli so that elements tended to lose their individuality (leveling) and an equally stable tendency in other individuals to highlight differences (sharpening). This organizing principle is apparent in judgments of the size of a series of objects, as well as in memory, where it may manifest itself in a blurring of elements in the recall of a story.

Another much studied cognitive control is called field dependence–field independence. It pertains to the extent to which people are influenced by inner (field-independent) or environmental (field-dependent) cues in orienting themselves in space and the extent to which they make fine differentiations in the environment. The more field-independent people are, the greater is their ability to articulate a field. There are no general intellectual capacity differences between field-dependent and field-independent people, but there is a tendency for field-dependent people to favour careers that include working with other people, such as teaching or social work. Field-independent people are more often found in careers that involve abstract issues such as mathematics. Cultural differences have also been found. Some Eskimo live and hunt in an environment with little variation, and a high degree of articulation of the field (field independence) would favour survival; some farmers of Sierra Leone, however, who inhabit an area of lush vegetation and many varieties of shape, require less differentiation of the field.

CHAPTER FIVE

INFLUENTIAL FIGURES IN PSYCHOLOGY

M ultiple people have shaped the field of psychology, and significant contributions continue to be made in the present day. What follows is merely a glance at the figures who have had the greatest impact on the field.

WILHELM WUNDT

(1832–1920)

Wilhelm Wundt was a German physiologist and psychologist who is generally acknowledged as the founder of experimental psychology. He was born near Mannheim, Ger., on Aug. 16, 1832. Wundt earned a medical degree at the University of Heidelberg in 1856. After studying briefly with Johannes Müller, he was appointed lecturer in physiology at the University of Heidelberg, where in 1858 he became an assistant to the physicist and physiologist Hermann von Helmholtz. There he wrote *Beiträge zur Theorie der Sinneswahrnehmung* (1858–62; *Contributions to the Theory of Sense Perception*).

It was during this period, in 1862, that Wundt offered the first course ever taught in scientific psychology. Until then, psychology had been regarded as a branch of philosophy and, hence, to be conducted primarily by rational analysis. Wundt instead stressed the use of experimental methods drawn from the natural sciences. His lectures on psychology were published as *Vorlesungen über die Menschen und Thierseele* (1863;

Wundt regarded description of the contents of consciousness as the proper focus of scientific psychology.

Lectures on the Mind of Humans and Animals). He was promoted to assistant professor of physiology in 1864.

Bypassed in 1871 for the appointment to succeed Helmholtz, Wundt then applied himself to writing a work that came to be one of the most important in the history of psychology, *Grundzüge der physiologischen Psychologie,* 2 vol. (1873–74; 3 vol., 6th ed., 1908–11; *Principles of Physiological Psychology*). The *Grundzüge* advanced a system of psychology that sought to investigate the immediate experiences of consciousness, including sensations, feelings, volitions, and ideas; it also contained the concept of apperception, or conscious perception. The methodology prescribed was introspection, or conscious examination of conscious experience.

In 1874 Wundt went to the University of Zürich for a year before embarking on the most productive phase of his career, as professor at the University of Leipzig (1875–1917). There, in 1879, he established the first psychological laboratory in the world, and two years later he founded the first journal of psychology, *Philosophische Studien (Philosophical Studies)*. Wundt's most important later works include *Grundriss der Psychologie* (1896; *Outline of Psychology*) and *Völkerpsychologie,* 10 vol. (1900–20; *Ethnic Psychology*). He died in Grossbothen, Ger., on Aug. 31, 1920.

WILLIAM JAMES

(1842–1910)

The American psychologist and philosopher William James had a remarkable variety of talents. Most notably he was a leader in the movement known as Pragmatism, which stresses that the meaning and value of any idea are to be explained in terms of its experiential consequences.

James was born on Jan. 11, 1842, in New York City. His early education, like that of his brother, the famous novelist Henry James, was varied. Although William's first ambition was to be an artist, he entered Harvard Medical School in 1864. He was granted a degree in medicine in 1869, but by that time had decided that he would not practice medicine. He had studied chemistry, comparative anatomy, and physiology. In 1865 he went on a geological expedition to Brazil with Swiss-American naturalist and teacher Louis Agassiz. James had also read widely in literature, history, and philosophy. He wrote literary criticism and became interested in psychology.

James was appointed an instructor in physiology at Harvard in 1872. He later taught psychology and philosophy and became famous as one of the outstanding teachers of his time. In 1884 the "James-Lange theory" was published. It set forth James's belief that emotions are organic sensations aroused by bodily expression—that we feel sorry because we cry, and angry because we strike. James's most important work, *The Principles of Psychology*, was published in 1890. In this book, James advocated the new psychology that acknowledged a kinship with science as well as with philosophy. The book immediately became popular with laymen as well as with psychologists.

James's increasing fame made him much in demand as a lecturer. He also wrote *The Varieties of Religious Experience,* published in 1902, and *Pragmatism: A New Name for Old Ways of Thinking* (1907). In 1907 James taught his last course at Harvard. He died three years later in Chocorua, N.H.

JOSEF BREUER

(1842–1925)

Josef Breuer was an Austrian physician and physiologist who was acknowledged by Sigmund Freud and others as the principal forerunner of psychoanalysis. Breuer found, in 1880, that he had relieved symptoms of hysteria in a patient, Bertha Pappenheim, called Anna O. in his case study, after he had induced her to recall unpleasant past experiences under hypnosis. He concluded that neurotic symptoms result from unconscious processes and will disappear when these processes become conscious. The case of Anna O. was important because it introduced Freud to the cathartic method (the "talking cure") that was pivotal in his later work.

Breuer described his methods and results to Freud and referred patients to him. With Freud he wrote *Studien über Hysterie* (1895; *Studies on Hysteria*), in which Breuer's treatment of hysteria was described. Later disagreement on basic theories of therapy terminated their collaboration.

G. STANLEY HALL

(1844–1924)

Psychologist G. Stanley Hall, in full Granville Stanley Hall, gave early impetus and direction to the development of psychology in the United States. Frequently regarded as the founder of child psychology and educational psychology, he also did much to direct into the psychological currents of his time the ideas of Charles Darwin, Sigmund Freud, and others.

Hall graduated from Williams College in 1867. Although he originally intended to enter the ministry, he left Union Theological Seminary in New York City after one year (1867–68) to study philosophy in Germany (1868–71). He became a lecturer at Antioch College in Ohio in 1872. His decision to adopt psychology as his life's work was inspired by a partial reading of *Physiological Psychology* (1873–74), by Wilhelm Wundt. Hall resigned his post at Antioch in 1876 and returned to Germany for further study, becoming acquainted with Wundt and the German physicist and physiologist Hermann von Helmholtz. There Hall discovered the value of the questionnaire

Hall played a key role in establishing the study of psychology in the United States.

for psychological research. Later he and his students devised more than 190 questionnaires, which were instrumental in stimulating the upsurge of interest in the study of child development.

After returning to the United States, Hall in 1878 earned from Harvard University the first Ph.D. in psychology granted in America. He then gave special lectures on education at Harvard, and he used questionnaires from a study of Boston schools to write two significant papers: one dealing with children's lies (1882) and the other with the contents of children's minds (1883).

A lectureship in philosophy (1883) and a professorship in psychology and pedagogics (1884) at Johns Hopkins University followed. There Hall was given space for one of the first psychological laboratories in the United States. The philosopher-psychologist-educator John Dewey was one of the first to use it. In 1887 Hall founded the *American Journal of Psychology*, the first such American journal and the second of any significance outside Germany.

At this point, Hall was entering the most influential period of his life. The following year (1888), he helped to establish Clark University in Worcester, Mass., and, as the university's president and a professor of psychology, he became a major force in shaping experimental psychology into a science. A great teacher, he inspired research that reached into all areas of psychology. By 1893 he had awarded 11 of the 14 doctorates in psychology granted in the United States. The first journal in the fields of child and educational psychology, the *Pedagogical Seminary* (later the *Journal of Genetic Psychology*), was founded by Hall in 1893.

Hall's theory that mental growth proceeds by evolutionary stages is best expressed in one of his largest and most important works, *Adolescence* (1904). Despite opposition, Hall, as an early proponent of psychoanalysis, invited Sigmund Freud and Carl Jung to the conferences celebrating Clark University's 20th anniversary (1909). Hall was a leading spirit in the founding of the American Psychological Association and served as its first president (1892).

IVAN PETROVICH PAVLOV

(1849–1936)

Although he was a brilliant physiologist and a skillful surgeon, Ivan Pavlov is remembered primarily for his development of the concept of conditioned reflex. In a well-known experiment he trained a hungry dog to salivate at the sound of a bell. The bell had previously become associated by the dog with the sight of food. Pavlov's work laid a foundation for the scientific analysis of human behavior. In 1904 he was awarded the Nobel Prize for Physiology or Medicine for his work on digestive secretions.

Pavlov was born in Ryazan, Russia. He attended a church school and later a theological seminary. In 1870 he abandoned his religious studies to go to the University of St. Petersburg to study chemistry and physiology. He received his doctorate in medicine from the Imperial Medical Academy in 1879 and pursued further schooling in Germany at Leipzig and Breslau. From 1888 to 1890 Pavlov investigated the structure of the human heart and the regulation of blood pressure. From 1890 to 1924 he was professor of physiology at the Imperial Medical Academy.

The years from 1890 to 1900 were spent analyzing the secretory activity of digestion in animals. Through his observations Pavlov was able to formulate the laws of conditioned reflex. This subject occupied much of his time until 1930. After 1930 he began to apply his laws to the study of human mental illnesses.

Pavlov was able to continue his work after the Russian Revolution of 1917 in spite of his persistent opposition to communism. Even under Joseph Stalin's rule he was not hindered in his experiments. During the last two years of his life Pavlov gradually stopped his criticisms, perhaps because of increased government support for his experimental projects.

SIGMUND FREUD

(1856–1939)

Sigmund Freud, an Austrian neurologist who was the founder of psychoanalysis, may justly be called the most influential intellectual of his age. The impact of his work remained powerful well after his death and in fields far removed from psychology as it is narrowly defined.

Freud's father, Jakob, was a Jewish wool merchant who had been married once before he wed the boy's mother, Amalie Nathansohn. His father, 40 years old at Freud's birth, seems to have been a relatively remote and authoritarian figure, while his mother appears to have been more nurturant and emotionally available. Although Freud had two older half-brothers, his strongest if also most ambivalent attachment seems to have been to a nephew, John, one year his senior, who provided the model of intimate friend and hated rival that Freud reproduced often at later stages of his life. In 1859 the Freud family was compelled for economic reasons to move to Leipzig and then a year after to Vienna, where Freud remained until the Nazi annexation of Austria 78 years later.

In 1873 Freud graduated from the Sperl Gymnasium and, apparently inspired by a public reading of an essay by Goethe on nature, turned to medicine as a career. At the University of Vienna he worked with one of the leading physiologists of his day, Ernst von Brücke, an exponent of the materialist, antivitalist science of Hermann von Helmholtz. In 1882 he entered the General Hospital in Vienna as a clinical assistant to train with the psychiatrist Theodor Meynert and the professor of internal medicine Hermann Nothnagel. In 1885 Freud was appointed lecturer in neuropathology, having concluded important research on the brain's medulla. Freud's scientific training remained of cardinal importance in his work, or at least in his own conception of it.

In late 1885 Freud went to the Salpêtrière clinic in Paris, where he worked under the guidance of Jean-Martin Charcot. His 19 weeks in

Freud's work became the foundation for treating psychiatric disorders by psychoanalysis.

the French capital proved a turning point in his career, for Charcot's work with patients classified as "hysterics" introduced Freud to the possibility that psychological disorders might have their source in the mind rather than the brain.

Freud later developed a partnership with the physician Josef Breuer after his return to Vienna from Paris. Freud turned to a clinical practice in neuropsychology, and the office he established at Berggasse 19 was to remain his consulting room for almost half a century. Before their collaboration began, during the early 1880s, Breuer had treated a patient named Bertha Pappenheim—or "Anna O.," as she became known in the literature—who was suffering from a variety of hysterical symptoms. Rather than using hypnotic suggestion, as had Charcot, Breuer allowed her to lapse into a state resembling autohypnosis, in which she would talk about the initial manifestations of her symptoms. To Breuer's surprise, the very act of verbalization seemed to provide some relief from their hold over her (although later scholarship has cast doubt on its permanence). "The talking cure" or "chimney sweeping," as Breuer and Anna O., respectively, called it, seemed to act cathartically to produce an abreaction, or discharge, of the pent-up emotional blockage at the root of the pathological behaviour.

Freud, still beholden to Charcot's hypnotic method, did not grasp the full implications of Breuer's experience until a decade later, when he developed the technique of free association. In part an extrapolation of the automatic writing promoted by the German Jewish writer Ludwig Börne a century before, in part a result of his own clinical experience with other hysterics, this revolutionary method was announced in the work Freud published jointly with Breuer in 1895, *Studien über Hysterie (Studies in Hysteria)*.

By encouraging the patient to express any random thoughts that came associatively to mind, the technique aimed at uncovering hitherto unarticulated material from the realm of the psyche that Freud, following a long tradition, called the unconscious. Difficulty in freely associating—sudden silences, stuttering, or the like—suggested to Freud the importance of the material struggling to be expressed, as well as the power of what he called the patient's defenses against that expression. Such blockages Freud dubbed resistance, which had to be broken down in order to reveal hidden conflicts. Unlike Charcot and Breuer, Freud came to the conclusion, based on his clinical experience with female hysterics, that the most insistent source of resisted material was sexual in nature. And even more momentously, he linked the etiology of neurotic symptoms to the same struggle between a sexual feeling or urge and the psychic defenses against it.

At first, however, Freud was uncertain about the precise status of the sexual component in this dynamic conception of the psyche. In a now famous letter to his close friend Wilhelm Fliess of Sept. 2, 1897, he concluded that, rather than being memories of actual events, these shocking recollections were the residues of infantile impulses and desires to be seduced by an adult. What was recalled was not a genuine memory but what he would later call a screen memory, or fantasy, hiding a primitive wish. That is, rather than stressing the corrupting initiative of adults in the etiology of neuroses, Freud concluded that the fantasies and yearnings of the child were at the root of later conflict.

In *Die Traumdeutung (The Interpretation of Dreams)*—published in 1899, but given the date of the dawning century to emphasize its epochal character—Freud interspersed evidence from his own dreams with evidence from those recounted in his clinical practice. He contended that dreams played a fundamental role in the psychic economy. The mind's energy—which Freud called libido and identified principally, but not exclusively, with the sexual drive—was a fluid and malleable force capable of excessive and disturbing power. Needing to be discharged to ensure pleasure and prevent pain, it sought whatever outlet it might find. If denied the gratification provided by direct motor action, libidinal energy could seek its release through mental channels. *The Interpretation of Dreams* provides a hermeneutic for the unmasking of the dream's disguise, or dreamwork, as Freud called it. The manifest content of the dream, that which is remembered and reported, must be understood as veiling a latent meaning. Dreams defy logical entailment and narrative coherence, for they intermingle the residues of immediate daily experience with the deepest, often most infantile wishes. Yet they can be ultimately decoded, and their mystifying effects can be reversed.

In 1904 Freud published *Zur Psychopathologie des Alltagslebens (The Psychopathology of Everyday Life)*, in which he explored such seemingly insignificant errors as slips of the tongue or pen (later colloquially called Freudian slips), misreadings, or forgetting of names. These errors Freud understood to have symptomatic and thus interpretable importance. But unlike dreams they need not betray a repressed infantile wish yet can arise from more immediate hostile, jealous, or egoistic causes.

In 1905 Freud extended the scope of this analysis by examining *Der Witz und seine Beziehung zum Unbewussten (Jokes and Their Relation to the Unconscious)*. Invoking the idea of "joke-work" as a process comparable to dreamwork, he also acknowledged the double-sided quality of jokes, at once consciously contrived and unconsciously revealing. Insofar as jokes are more deliberate than dreams or slips, they draw on the rational dimension of the psyche that Freud was to call the ego as much as on what he was to call the id. Also in that year, Freud published the work that first thrust him into the limelight as the alleged champion of a sexual understanding of the mind. *Drei Abhandlungen zur Sexualtheorie (Three Contributions to the Sexual Theory*, later translated as *Three Essays on the Theory of Sexuality)* outlined in greater detail than before his reasons for emphasizing the sexual component in the development of both normal and pathological behaviour.

According to Freud, an originally unfocused sexuality first seeks gratification orally through sucking at the mother's breast. Initially unable to distinguish between self and breast, the infant soon comes to appreciate its mother as the first external love object. After the oral phase, during the second year, the child's focus shifts to its anus, stimulated by the struggle over toilet training. During the anal phase the child's pleasure in defecation is confronted with the demands of self-control. The third phase, lasting from about the fourth to the sixth year, he

Id, Ego, and Superego

Freud's topographical division of the psyche into the unconscious, preconscious, and conscious was superceded by his later structural categorization into id, ego, and superego. The id was defined in terms of the most primitive urges for gratification in the infant, urges dominated by the desire for pleasure through the release of tension and invested energy. The id is ruled by what Freud called the primary process directly expressing bodily generated instincts. The secondary process that results leads to the growth of the ego, which follows what Freud called the reality principle in contrast to the pleasure principle dominating the id.

The last component in Freud's trichotomy, the superego, develops from the internalization of society's moral commands through identification with parental dictates. Only partly conscious, the superego gains some of its punishing force by borrowing certain aggressive elements in the id, which are turned inward against the ego and produce feelings of guilt. But it is largely through the internalization of social norms that the superego is constituted, an acknowledgement that prevents psychoanalysis from conceptualizing the psyche in purely biologistic or individualistic terms.

Freud's understanding of the primary process underwent a crucial shift in the course of his career. Initially he counterposed a libidinal drive that seeks sexual pleasure to a self-preservation drive whose telos is survival. But in 1914, while examining the phenomenon of narcissism, he came to consider the latter instinct as merely a variant of the former. Unable to accept so monistic a drive theory, Freud sought a new dualistic alternative. He arrived at the speculative assertion that there exists in the psyche an innate, regressive drive for stasis that aims to end life's inevitable tension. This striving for rest he christened the Nirvana principle and the drive underlying it the death instinct, or Thanatos, which he could substitute for self-preservation as the contrary of the life instinct, or Eros.

called the phallic. Because Freud relied on male sexuality as the norm of development, his analysis of this phase aroused considerable opposition, especially because he claimed its major concern is castration anxiety.

In addition to the neurosis of hysteria, with its conversion of emotional conflicts into bodily symptoms, Freud developed complicated explanations of other typical neurotic behaviour, such as obsessive-compulsions, paranoia, and narcissism. These he called psychoneuroses, because of their rootedness in childhood conflicts, as opposed to the actual neuroses such as hypochondria, neurasthenia, and anxiety neurosis, which are due to problems in the present (the last, for example, being caused by the physical suppression of sexual release).

Freud developed the celebrated technique of having the patient lie on a couch, not looking directly at the analyst, and free to fantasize with as little intrusion of the analyst's real personality as possible. Restrained and neutral, the analyst functions as a screen for the displacement of early emotions, both erotic and aggressive. This transference onto the analyst is itself a kind of neurosis, but one in the service of an ultimate working through of the conflicting feelings it expresses. Only certain illnesses, however, are open to this treatment, for it demands the ability to redirect libidinal energy outward. The psychoses, Freud sadly concluded, are based on the redirection of libido back onto the patient's ego and cannot therefore be relieved by transference in the analytic situation. How successful psychoanalytic therapy has been in the treatment of psychoneuroses remains, however, a matter of considerable dispute.

Although Freud's theories were offensive to many in the Vienna of his day, they began to attract a cosmopolitan group of supporters in the early 1900s.

Freud was Jewish, and when the Nazis invaded Austria in 1938, they burned his books and banned his theories. Friends got him out of Austria to England. He died of cancer of the jaw and palate in London on Sept. 23, 1939.

ALFRED ADLER

(1870–1937)

The Austrian psychiatrist Alfred Adler developed the influential system of individual psychology that introduced the term *inferiority feeling* (later widely and often inaccurately called inferiority complex). Adler worked to create a flexible, supportive psychotherapy to direct those emotionally disabled by inferiority feelings toward maturity, common sense, and social usefulness.

Throughout his life Adler maintained a strong awareness of social problems, and this served as a principal motivation in his work. From his earliest years as a physician (M.D., University of Vienna Medical School, 1895), he stressed consideration of the patient in relation to the total environment, and he began developing a humanistic, holistic approach to human problems.

About 1900 Adler began to explore psychopathology within the context of general medicine and in 1902 became closely associated with Sigmund Freud. Gradually, however, differences between the two became irreconcilable, notably after the appearance of Adler's *Studie über Minderwertigkeit von Organen* (1907; *Study of Organ Inferiority and*

Adler's theories influenced educators, as well as many
other psychologists and psychiatrists.

Its Psychical Compensation), in which he suggested that persons try to compensate psychologically for a physical disability and its attendant feeling of inferiority. Unsatisfactory compensation results in neurosis. Adler increasingly downplayed Freud's basic contention that sexual conflicts in early childhood cause mental illness, and he further came to confine sexuality to a symbolic role in human strivings to overcome feelings of inadequacy. Outspokenly critical of Freud by 1911, Adler and a group of followers severed ties with Freud's circle and began developing what they called individual psychology, first outlined in *Über den nervösen Charakter* (1912; *The Neurotic Constitution*). The system was elaborated in later editions of this work and in other writings, such as *Menschenkenntnis* (1927; *Understanding Human Nature*).

Individual psychology maintains that the overriding motivation in most people is a striving for what Adler somewhat misleadingly termed superiority (i.e., self-realization, completeness, or perfection). This striving for superiority may be frustrated by feelings of inferiority, inadequacy, or incompleteness arising from physical defects, low social status, pampering or neglect during childhood, or other causes encountered in the course of life. Individuals can compensate for their feelings of inferiority by developing their skills and abilities, or, less healthily, they may develop an inferiority complex that comes to dominate their behaviour. Overcompensation for inferiority feelings can take the form of an egocentric striving for power and self-aggrandizing behaviour at others' expense.

Each person develops his personality and strives for perfection in his own particular way, in what Adler termed a style of life, or lifestyle. The individual's lifestyle forms in early childhood and is partly determined by what particular inferiority affected him most deeply during his formative years. The striving for superiority coexists with another innate urge: to cooperate and work with other people for the common good, a drive that Adler termed the social interest. Mental health is characterized by reason, social interest, and self-transcendence; mental disorder by feelings of inferiority and self-centred concern for one's safety and superiority or power over others. The Adlerian psychotherapist directs the patient's attention to the unsuccessful, neurotic character of his attempts to cope with feelings of inferiority. Once the patient has become aware of these, the therapist builds up his self-esteem, helps him adopt more realistic goals, and encourages more useful behaviour and a stronger social interest.

In 1921 Adler established the first child-guidance clinic in Vienna, soon thereafter opening and maintaining about 30 more there under his direction. Adler first went to the United States in 1926 and became visiting professor at Columbia University in 1927. He was appointed visiting professor of the Long Island College of Medicine in New York in 1932.

ÉDOUARD CLAPARÈDE

(1873–1940)

The Swiss psychologist Édouard Claparède is particularly remembered for his formulation of the law of momentary interest, a fundamental tenet of psychology stating that thinking is a biological activity in service to the human organism. He conducted exploratory research in the fields of child psychology, educational psychology, concept formation, problem solving, and sleep.

After completing his medical studies (1897), Claparède spent a year in research in Paris, where he met Alfred Binet, a major developer of intelligence testing. After returning to Geneva, he joined the laboratory of his psychologist cousin, Theodore Flournoy, and began lecturing at the University of Geneva. About this time he became interested in comparative, that is, animal psychology.

In 1905 Claparède advanced a biological theory of sleep that anticipated the views of Sigmund Freud. He considered sleep to be a defensive reaction to halt activity of the organism and thereby prevent exhaustion. His research on sleep led him to the study of hysteria and the conclusion that hysterical symptoms may also be regarded as defensive reactions. After the appearance of his influential book *Experimental Pedagogy and the Psychology of the Child* (1905; Eng. trans., 1911), he began to conduct a seminar in educational psychology (1906). Advancing to professor of psychology (1908), he established the Institut J.J. Rousseau for the advancement of child psychology and its application to education (1912).

CARL JUNG

(1875–1961)

Carl Jung was a Swiss psychologist and psychiatrist who was the founder of analytic psychology—in some aspects a response to Sigmund Freud's psychoanalysis. Jung proposed and developed the concepts of the extraverted and the introverted personality, archetypes, and the collective unconscious. His work has been influential in psychiatry and in the study of religion, literature, and related fields.

Jung was the son of a philologist and pastor. His childhood was lonely, although enriched by a vivid imagination, and from an early age he observed the behaviour of his parents and teachers, which he tried to resolve. Especially concerned with his father's failing belief in religion, he tried to communicate to him his own experience of God. In many ways, the elder Jung was a kind and tolerant man, but neither he nor his son succeeded in understanding each other. Jung seemed destined to become a minister, for there were a number of clergymen on both sides of his family. In his teens he discovered philosophy and read widely, and this, together with the disappointments of his boyhood, led him to forsake the strong family tradition and to study medicine and become a psychiatrist. He was a student at the universities of Basel (1895–1900) and Zürich (M.D., 1902).

He was fortunate in joining the staff of the Burghölzli Asylum of the University of Zürich at a time (1900) when it was under the

118

Jung emphasized the analysis of current problems, rather than childhood conflicts, in the treatment of adults.

direction of Eugen Bleuler, whose psychological interests had initiated what are now considered classical studies of mental illness. At Burghölzli, Jung began, with outstanding success, to apply association tests initiated by earlier researchers. He studied, especially, patients' peculiar and illogical responses to stimulus words and found that they were caused by emotionally charged clusters of associations withheld from consciousness because of their disagreeable, immoral (to them), and frequently sexual content. He used the now famous term *complex* to describe such conditions.

These researches, which established him as a psychiatrist of international repute, led him to understand Freud's investigations; his findings confirmed many of Freud's ideas, and, for a period of five years (between 1907 and 1912), he was Freud's close collaborator. He held important positions in the psychoanalytic movement and was widely thought of as the most likely successor to the founder of psychoanalysis. But this was not to be the outcome of their relationship. Partly for temperamental reasons and partly because of differences of viewpoint, the collaboration ended. At this stage Jung differed with Freud largely over the latter's insistence on the sexual bases of neurosis. A serious disagreement came in 1912, with the publication of Jung's *Wandlungen und Symbole der Libido (Psychology of the Unconscious, 1916)*, which ran counter to many of Freud's ideas. Although Jung had been elected president of the International Psychoanalytic Society in 1911, he resigned from the society in 1914.

His first achievement was to differentiate two classes of people according to attitude types: extraverted (outward-looking) and introverted (inward-looking). Later he differentiated four functions of the mind—thinking, feeling, sensation, and intuition—one or more of which predominate in any given person. Results of this study were embodied in *Psychologische Typen* (1921; *Psychological Types,* 1923). Jung's wide scholarship was well manifested here, as it also had been in *The Psychology of the Unconscious.*

As a boy Jung had remarkably striking dreams and powerful fantasies that had developed with unusual intensity. After his break with Freud, he deliberately allowed this aspect of himself to function again and gave the irrational side of his nature free expression. At the same time, he studied it scientifically by keeping detailed notes of his strange experiences. He later developed the theory that these experiences came from an area of the mind that he called the collective unconscious, which he held was shared by everyone. This much-contested conception was combined with a theory of archetypes that Jung held as fundamental to the study of the psychology of religion.

INTROVERT AND EXTRAVERT

Introvert and extravert are the two basic personality types distinguished by the Swiss psychiatrist Carl Jung. According to Jung, an introvert is a person whose interest is generally directed inward toward his own feelings and thoughts, in contrast to an extravert, whose attention is directed toward other people and the outside world. The typical introvert is shy, contemplative, and reserved and tends to have difficulty adjusting to social situations. Excessive daydreaming and introspection, careful balancing of considerations before reaching decisions, and withdrawal under stress are also typical of the introverted personality. The extravert, by contrast, is characterized by outgoingness, responsiveness to other persons, activity, aggressiveness, and the ability to make quick decisions.

This typology is now regarded as simplistic because almost no one can be accurately described as wholly introverted or extraverted. Most people fall somewhere between Jung's two types—i.e., they are ambiverts, in whom introversive and extraversive tendencies exist in a rough balance and are manifested at different times in response to different situations.

In Jung's terms, archetypes are instinctive patterns, have a universal character, and are expressed in behaviour and images.

Jung devoted the rest of his life to developing his ideas, especially those on the relation between psychology and religion. In his view, obscure and often neglected texts of writers in the past shed unexpected light not only on Jung's own dreams and fantasies but also on those of his patients; he thought it necessary for the successful practice of their art that psychotherapists become familiar with writings of the old masters.

Besides the development of new psychotherapeutic methods that derived from his own experience and the theories developed from them, Jung gave fresh importance to the so-called Hermetic tradition. He conceived that the Christian religion was part of a historic process necessary for the development of consciousness, and he also thought that the heretical movements, starting with Gnosticism and ending in alchemy, were manifestations of unconscious archetypal elements not adequately expressed in the mainstream forms of Christianity. He was particularly impressed with his finding that alchemical-like symbols could be found frequently in modern dreams and fantasies, and he thought that alchemists had constructed a kind of textbook of the collective unconscious. He expounded on this in 4 out of the 18 volumes that make up his *Collected Works*.

Jung's historical studies aided him in pioneering the psychotherapy of the middle-aged and elderly, in particular those who felt that their lives had lost meaning. He helped them to appreciate the place of their lives in the sequence of history. Most of these patients had lost their religious belief; he found that if they could discover their own myth as expressed in dream and imagination they would become more complete personalities. Jung referred to this process as individuation.

In later years he became professor of psychology at the Federal Polytechnical University in Zürich (1933–41) and professor of medical psychology at the University of Basel (1943). His personal experience, his continued psychotherapeutic practice, and his wide knowledge of history placed him in a unique position to comment on current events. As early as 1918 he had begun to think that Germany held a special position in Europe; the Nazi revolution was, therefore, highly significant for him, and he delivered a number of hotly contested views that led to his being wrongly branded as a Nazi sympathizer. Jung lived to the age of 85.

JOHN B. WATSON
(1878–1958)

John Broadus Watson was an American psychologist who codified and publicized behaviourism, an approach to psychology that, in his view, was restricted to the objective, experimental study of the relations between environmental events and human behaviour. Watsonian behaviourism became the dominant psychology in the United States during the 1920s and '30s.

Watson received his Ph.D. in psychology from the University of Chicago (1903), where he then taught. In 1908 he became professor of psychology at Johns Hopkins University in Baltimore, Md., and immediately established a laboratory for research in comparative, or animal, psychology. He articulated his first statements on behaviourist psychology in the epoch-making article "Psychology as a Behaviorist Views It" (1913), claiming that psychology is the science of human behaviour, which, like animal behaviour, should be studied under exacting laboratory conditions.

His first major work, *Behavior: An Introduction to Comparative Psychology*, was published in 1914. In it he argued forcefully for the use of animal subjects in psychological study and described instinct as a series of reflexes activated by heredity. He also promoted conditioned responses as the ideal experimental tool. In 1918 Watson ventured into the relatively unexplored field of infant study. In one of his classic experiments, he conditioned fear of white rats and other furry objects in an 11-month-old boy.

The definitive statement of Watson's position appears in another major work, *Psychology from the Standpoint of a Behaviorist* (1919), in which he sought to extend the principles and methods of comparative psychology to the study of human beings and staunchly advocated the use of conditioning in research. His association with academic psychology ended abruptly. In 1920, in the wake of sensational publicity surrounding his divorce from his first wife, Watson resigned from Johns Hopkins. He entered the advertising business in 1921.

Watson's book *Behaviorism* (1925), for the general reader, is credited with interesting many in entering professional psychology. Following *Psychological Care of Infant and Child* (1928) and his revision (1930) of *Behaviorism*, Watson devoted himself exclusively to business until his retirement (1946).

CLARK L. HULL

(1884–1952)

American psychologist Clark Leonard Hull is known for his experimental studies on learning and for his attempt to give mathematical expression to psychological theory. He applied a deductive method of reasoning similar to that used in geometry, proposing that a series of postulates about psychology could be developed, from which logical conclusions could be deduced and tested.

As a student at the University of Michigan at Ann Arbor, Hull became interested in psychology, receiving his Ph.D. from the University of Wisconsin, Madison, in 1918. He then joined the faculty at Wisconsin and worked on the prediction and measurement of aptitude, which led to his first major publication, *Aptitude Testing* (1928). He became interested in hypnosis, conducting experiments in the field after joining the Institute of Human Relations at Yale University in 1929. The results of his rigorous scientific studies formed the basis of *Hypnosis and Suggestibility* (1933).

During his early years at Yale, Hull began to formulate his global theory of behaviour, which he based on principles drawn from a variety of sources. He took certain ideas on conditioning from the Russian physiologist Ivan Pavlov and also borrowed from American psychologists, including John B. Watson, who emphasized the objective study of behaviour, and Edward L. Thorndike, who asserted the importance of reinforcement in learning.

The reinforcement theory of learning formed the basis for most of Hull's work. The theory explains behaviour in terms of stimulus and response, which become associated with each other in the learning process. The tendency for an association to be made is strengthened when reinforcement is given, that is, when the response reduces a physiological or psychological need. When a need such as hunger is less strong, as when an animal in a laboratory test is satiated, the reinforcement (for example, food) has less effect and the animal performs less well on learning tasks. On the other hand, Hull hypothesized that animals would learn more quickly the stronger the physiological need or drive and the more immediate the reward or reinforcement; this he later confirmed by experiment. Complex behaviour could be explained by a series of such simple response mechanisms, according to Hull.

Hull believed that psychology had its own quantitative laws that could be stated in mathematical equations. He further developed these ideas in *Principles of Behavior* (1943), which suggested that the stimulus-response connection depends on both the kind and the amount of reinforcement.

WOLFGANG KÖHLER

(1887–1967)

The German psychologist Wolfgang Köhler was a key figure in the development of Gestalt psychology, which seeks to understand learning, perception, and other components of mental life as structured wholes.

Köhler's doctoral thesis with Carl Stumpf at the University of Berlin (1909) was an investigation of hearing. As assistant and lecturer at the University of Frankfurt (1911), he continued his auditory research. In 1912 he and Kurt Koffka were subjects for experiments on perception conducted by Max Wertheimer, whose report on the experiments launched the Gestalt movement. Thereafter Köhler was associated with Wertheimer and Koffka as the three worked to gain acceptance for the new theory.

As director of the anthropoid research station of the Prussian Academy of Sciences at Tenerife, Canary Islands (1913–20), Köhler conducted experiments on problem solving by chimpanzees, revealing their ability to devise and use simple tools and build simple structures. His findings appeared in the classic *Intelligenzprüfungen an Menschenaffen* (1917; *The Mentality of Apes*), a work that emphasized insight and led to a radical revision of learning theory. Another major work, *Die physischen Gestalten in Ruhe und im stationären Zustand* (1920; *Physical Gestalt in Rest and Stationary States*), was based on an attempt to determine the relation of physical processes in nervous tissue to perception.

In 1921 Köhler became head of the psychological institute and professor of philosophy at the University of Berlin, directing a series of investigations that explored many aspects of Gestalt theory and publishing *Gestalt Psychology* in 1929. Outspoken in his criticism of Adolf Hitler's government, Köhler immigrated to the United States in 1935 and was professor of psychology at Swarthmore College, in Pennsylvania, until 1955.

ANNA FREUD

(1895–1982)

The Austrian-born British founder of child psychoanalysis and one of its foremost practitioners, Anna Freud also made fundamental contributions to understanding how the ego, or consciousness, functions in averting painful ideas, impulses, and feelings.

The youngest daughter of Sigmund Freud, Anna enjoyed an intimate association with developing psychoanalytic theory and practice. As a young woman she taught elementary school, and her daily observation of children drew her to child psychology. While serving as chairman of the Vienna Psycho-Analytic Society (1925–28), she published a paper (1927) outlining her approach to child psychoanalysis.

Publication of Anna Freud's *Das Ich und die Abwehrmechanismen* (1936; *The Ego and Mechanisms of Defense*, 1937) gave a strong, new impetus to ego psychology. The principal human defense mechanism, she indicated, is repression, an unconscious process that develops as the young child learns that some impulses, if acted upon, could prove dangerous to himself. Other mechanisms she described include the projection of one's own feeling into another; directing aggressive impulses against the self (suicide being the extreme example); identification with an overpowering aggressor; and the divorce of ideas from feelings. The work also was a pioneer effort in the development of adolescent psychology.

In 1938 Anna Freud and her father, whom she had cared for during a number of years of his terminal illness, escaped from Nazi-dominated Austria and settled in London, where she worked at a Hampstead nursery until 1945. During World War II she and a U.S. associate, Dorothy Burlingham, recounted their work in *Young Children in Wartime* (1942), *Infants Without Families* (1943), and *War and Children* (1943).

Anna Freud founded the Hampstead Child Therapy Course and Clinic, London, in 1947 and served as its director from 1952 to 1982. She viewed play as the child's adaptation to reality but not necessarily as a revelation of unconscious conflicts. She worked closely with parents and believed that analysis should have an educational influence on the child. A summation of her thought is to be found in her *Normality and Pathology in Childhood* (1968).

JEAN PIAGET

(1896–1980)

The Swiss psychologist Jean Piaget was the first to make a systematic study of the acquisition of understanding in children. He is thought by many to have been the major figure in 20th-century developmental psychology.

Piaget was an exceptionally intelligent child. By age 10 he had already published an article on zoology, his first scientific interest. At age 15 his articles had earned him a favorable reputation among European zoologists. He studied zoology and philosophy at the University of Neuchâtel and earned his doctorate in 1918. In philosophy he had studied epistemology, the theory of knowledge. He decided to combine this field with his background in biology and take up psychology. He went to Zürich to study under Carl Jung and Eugen Bleuler. This was followed by two years of work at the Sorbonne in Paris, beginning in 1919.

In Paris Piaget devised and administered reading tests to schoolchildren and became interested in the types of errors they made, leading him to explore the reasoning process in these young children. By 1921 he had begun to publish his findings; the same year brought him back to Switzerland, where he was appointed director of the Institut J.J. Rousseau in Geneva. In 1925–29 he was a professor at the University of Neuchâtel, and in 1929 he joined the faculty of the University of Geneva as professor of child psychology, remaining there until his death. In 1955 he established the International Centre of Genetic Epistemology at Geneva and became its director. His interests included scientific thought, sociology, and experimental psychology. In more than 50 books and monographs over his long career, Piaget continued to develop the theme he had first discovered in Paris, that the mind of the child evolves through a series of set stages to adulthood.

Piaget saw the child as constantly creating and re-creating his own model of reality, achieving mental growth by integrating simpler concepts into higher-level concepts at each stage, tracing four stages in that development. He described the child during the first two years of life as being in a sensorimotor stage, chiefly concerned with mastering his own innate physical reflexes and extending them into pleasurable or interesting actions. During the same period, the child first becomes aware of himself as a separate physical entity and then realizes that the objects

Piaget, seen here observing a class, viewed children as people who continually make and remake their own reality.

around him also have a separate and permanent existence. In the second, or preoperational, stage, roughly from age 2 to age 6 or 7, the child learns to manipulate his environment symbolically through inner representations, or thoughts, about the external world. During this stage he learns to represent objects by words and to manipulate the words mentally, just as he earlier manipulated the physical objects themselves. In the third, or concrete operational, stage, from age 7 to age 11 or 12, occur the beginning of logic in the child's thought processes and the beginning of the classification of objects by their similarities and differences. During this period the child also begins to grasp concepts of time and number. The fourth stage, the period of formal operations, begins at age 12 and extends into adulthood. It is characterized by an orderliness of thinking and a mastery of logical thought, allowing a more flexible kind of mental experimentation. The child learns to manipulate abstract ideas, make hypotheses, and see the implications of his own thinking and that of others.

Piaget's concept of these developmental stages caused a reevaluation of older ideas of the child, of learning, and of education. If the development of certain thought processes was on a genetically determined timetable, simple reinforcement was not sufficient to teach concepts; the child's mental development would have to be at the proper stage to assimilate those concepts. Thus, the teacher became not a transmitter of knowledge but a guide to the child's own discovery of the world.

Piaget reached his conclusions about child development through his observations of and conversations with his own children, as well as others. He asked them ingenious and revealing questions about simple problems he had devised, and then he formed a picture of their way of viewing the world by analyzing their mistaken responses.

Among Piaget's major works are *Le Langage et la pensée chez l'enfant* (1923; *The Language and Thought of the Child*), *Le Jugement et la raisonnement chez l'enfant* (1924; *Judgment and Reasoning in the Child*), and *La Naissance de l'intelligence chez l'enfant* (1948; *The Origins of Intelligence in Children*).

ERIK H. ERIKSON

(1902–1994)

Erik Homburger Erikson was a German-born American psychoanalyst whose writings on social psychology, individual identity, and the interactions of psychology with history, politics, and culture influenced professional approaches to psycho-social problems and attracted much popular interest.

As a young man, Erikson attended art school and travelled around Europe. In 1927, when he was invited by the psychoanalyst Anna Freud to teach art, history, and geography at a small private school in Vienna, he entered psychoanalysis with her and underwent training to become a psychoanalyst himself. He became interested in the treatment of children and published his first paper in 1930, before completing psychoanalytic training and being elected to the Vienna Psychoanalytic Institute in 1933. The same year, he immigrated to the United States, where he practiced child psychoanalysis in Boston and joined the faculty of the Harvard Medical School. He became interested in studying the way the ego, or consciousness, operates creatively in sane, well-ordered individuals.

Erikson left Harvard in 1936 to join the Institute of Human Relations at Yale. Two years later he began his first studies of cultural influences on psychological development, working with Sioux Indian children at the Pine Ridge Reservation in South Dakota. These studies, and later work with the anthropologist Alfred Kroeber among the Yurok Indians of northern California, eventually contributed to Erikson's theory that all societies develop institutions to accommodate personality development but that the typical solutions to similar problems arrived at by different societies are different.

Erikson moved his clinical practice to San Francisco in 1939 and became professor of psychology at the University of California, Berkeley, in 1942. During the 1940s he produced the essays that were collected

Erikson coined the term *identity crisis*.

in *Childhood and Society* (1950), the first major exposition of his views on psychosocial development. The evocative work was edited by his wife, Joan Serson Erikson. Erikson conceived eight stages of development, each confronting the individual with his or her own psychosocial demands, which continued into old age. Personality development, according to Erikson, takes place through a series of identity crises that must be overcome and internalized by the individual in preparation for the next developmental stage.

Refusing to sign a loyalty oath required by the University of California in 1950, Erikson resigned his post and that year joined the Austen Riggs Center in Stockbridge, Mass. He then returned to Harvard as a lecturer and professor (1960–70) and professor emeritus (from 1970 until his death).

B.F. SKINNER

(1904–1990)

The American psychologist Burrhus Frederic Skinner was an influential exponent of behaviourism, a school which views human behaviour in terms of responses to environmental stimuli and favours the controlled, scientific study of responses as the most direct means of elucidating human nature.

Skinner was attracted to psychology through the work of the Russian physiologist Ivan Petrovich Pavlov on conditioned reflexes, articles on behaviourism by Bertrand Russell, and the ideas of John B. Watson, the founder of behaviourism. After receiving his Ph.D. from Harvard University (1931), he remained there as a researcher until 1936, when he joined the faculty of the University of Minnesota, Minneapolis, where he wrote *The Behavior of Organisms* (1938).

As professor of psychology at Indiana University, Bloomington (1945–48), Skinner gained some measure of public attention through his invention of the Air Crib baby tender—a large, soundproof, germ-free, mechanical, air-conditioned box designed to provide an optimal environment for child growth during the first two years of life. In 1948 he published one of his most controversial works, *Walden Two*, a novel on life in a utopian community modelled on his own principles of social engineering.

As a professor of psychology at Harvard University from 1948 (emeritus 1974), Skinner influenced a generation of psychologists. Using various kinds of experimental equipment that he devised, he trained laboratory animals to perform complex and sometimes quite exceptional actions. A striking example was his pigeons that learned to play table tennis. One of his best-known inventions, the Skinner box, has been adopted in pharmaceutical research for observing how drugs may modify animal behaviour.

His experiences in the step-by-step training of research animals led Skinner to formulate the principles of programmed learning, which he envisioned to be accomplished through the use of so-called teaching machines. Central to his approach is the concept of reinforcement, or reward. The student, learning by use of the machine at his own pace, is rewarded for responding correctly to questions about the material he is trying to master. Learning is thereby presumably reinforced and facilitated.

In addition to his widely read *Science and Human Behavior* (1953), Skinner wrote many other books, including *Verbal Behavior* (1957), *The Analysis of Behavior* (with J.G. Holland, 1961), and *Technology of Teaching* (1968). Another work that generated considerable controversy, *Beyond Freedom and Dignity* (1971), argued that concepts of freedom and dignity may lead to self-destruction and advanced the cause of a technology of behaviour comparable to that of the physical and biological sciences. Skinner published an autobiography in three parts: *Particulars of My Life* (1976), *The Shaping of a Behaviorist* (1979), and *A Matter of Consequences* (1983). The year before his death, *Recent Issues in the Analysis of Behavior* (1989) was published.

ALBERT BANDURA
(born 1925)

A Canadian-born American psychologist and originator of social cognitive theory, Albert Bandura is probably best known for his modeling study on aggression, which demonstrated that children can learn behaviours through the observation of adults.

After graduating from high school in 1946, Bandura pursued a bachelor's degree at the University of British Columbia and then did graduate work at the University of Iowa, where he received a master's degree in psychology (1951) and a doctorate in clinical psychology (1952).

In 1953 Bandura accepted a one-year instructorship at Stanford University, where he quickly secured a professorship. In 1974 he was named the David Starr Jordan Professor of Social Science in Psychology, and two years later he became chairman of the psychology department. He remained at Stanford for the rest of his career.

In 1961 Bandura carried out his famous Bobo doll experiment, a study in which researchers physically and verbally abused a clown-faced inflatable toy in front of preschool-age children, which led the children to later mimic the behaviour of the adults by attacking the doll in the same fashion. Subsequent experiments in which children were exposed to such violence on videotape yielded similar results.

In the late 1960s, prompted by the media's graphic coverage of the assassination of U.S. Sen. Robert F. Kennedy together with increased reports of children incurring serious injuries during attempted replications of dangerous behaviours depicted in television advertisements, the potential effects of television violence on children became a growing public concern. Owing to his related research, Bandura was invited to testify before the Federal Trade Commission (FTC), the Eisenhower Commission, and several congressional committees as to the evidence that televised violence affects aggressive behaviour. His testimony played a role in the FTC's decision to render as unacceptable portrayals of children engaging in risky activities—such as pounding one another in the head with mallets in an advertisement for headache medication—and subsequently to pass new advertising standards.

Bandura was the first to demonstrate (1977) that self-efficacy, or the belief in one's own capabilities, has an effect on what an individual chooses to do, the amount of effort he puts into doing it, and the way he feels as he is doing it. Bandura also discovered that learning occurs both through those beliefs and through social modelling—thereby originating social cognitive theory (1986), which holds that an individual's environment, cognition, and behaviour all interact to determine how he functions, as opposed to one of those factors playing a dominant role.

DANIEL KAHNEMAN

(born 1934)

An Israeli-born psychologist, Daniel Kahneman was a corecipient of the Nobel Prize for Economics in 2002 for his integration of psychological research into economic science. His pioneering work examined human judgment and decision making under uncertainty. Kahneman shared the award with American economist Vernon L. Smith.

Kahneman studied psychology at Hebrew University (B.A., 1954) in Jerusalem and the University of California, Berkeley (Ph.D., 1961). He was a lecturer (1961–70) and a professor (1970–78) of psychology at Hebrew University; from 2000 he held a fellowship at that university's Center for Rationality. After teaching at the University of British Columbia in Vancouver (1978–86) and the University of California, Berkeley (1986–94), Kahneman in 1993 became the Eugene Higgins Professor of Psychology at Princeton University and a professor of public affairs at Princeton's Woodrow Wilson School of Public and International Affairs, eventually retiring as emeritus professor of both posts in 2007. He was on the editorial boards of several academic journals, notably the *Journal of Behavioral Decision Making* and the *Journal of Risk and Uncertainty*.

Kahneman began his prizewinning research in the late 1960s. In order to increase understanding of how people make economic decisions, he drew on cognitive psychology in relation to the mental processes used in forming judgments and making choices. Kahneman's research with Amos Tversky on decision making under uncertainty resulted in the formulation of a new branch of economics, prospect theory, which was the subject of their seminal article *Prospect Theory: An Analysis of Decisions Under Risk* (1979). Previously, economists had believed that people's decisions are determined by the expected gains from each possible future scenario multiplied by its probability of occurring, but if people make an irrational judgment by giving more weight to some scenarios than to others, their decision will be different from that predicted by traditional economic theory. Kahneman's research (based on surveys and experiments) showed that his subjects were incapable of analyzing complex decision situations when the future consequences were uncertain. Instead, they relied on heuristic shortcuts, or rule of thumb, with few people evaluating their underlying probability.

In 2011 Kahneman received the Talcott Parsons Prize from the American Academy of Arts and Sciences for his contributions to the social sciences. Also that year he published the best-selling book *Thinking, Fast and Slow*, which provided an adept distillation of his work. In 2013 he was awarded the U.S. Presidential Medal of Freedom.

CONCLUSION

In the time since psychology emerged as a formal discipline in the late nineteenth century, its approach, focus, and methods have constantly evolved. The field continues its evolution today, with advances in science and technology driving much of the research. By the end of the twentieth century, cognitive psychology had become increasingly tied to neuroscience because of the development of new brain-measuring techniques such as functional magnetic resonance imaging, which allowed psychologists to observe brain activity accompanying the performance of various experimental tasks. Developmental, social, and clinical psychology also became increasingly concerned with brain processes. For example, diagnostic imaging has been used to discern a wide array of traits, including racism, altruism, aggression, and empathy.

The rise of neuroscience in psychological research was aided by the development of computational models that were much more neurologically realistic than earlier rule-based and connectionist ones, taking into account the firing behaviour of large populations of neurons in specific regions of the brain. Decision making, for example, involves interactions between areas responsible for high-level reasoning, such as the prefrontal cortex, and those associated with emotion, such as the amygdala.

Like neuroscience, genetics has made a major impact on the study of psychology. Epigenetics has become one of the most fertile areas of research in recent years. Its findings have implications for not just our understanding of behaviour, cognition, memory, and personality, but also for clinical psychology.

Psychology has a rich past and an exciting future. Its interdisciplinary nature gives it many directions in which it can grow, while its focus—how we think and behave—ensures a broad interest in the field.

ALGORITHM A procedure for solving a mathematical problem or accomplishing a goal that uses a limited number of steps and that often repeats sets of steps.

ANALYTIC PSYCHOLOGY The psychoanalytic method of Swiss psychiatrist Carl Jung, who attached less importance than did Freud to the role of sexuality in the origin of neuroses and who stressed the analysis of patients' immediate conflicts rather than those in childhood.

ANTHROPOLOGY A science that deals with human beings and especially with their physical characteristics, origin, environmental and social relations, and culture.

BEHAVIOURISM A school of psychology that relies exclusively on directly measurable and observable data and rejects the study of so-called inner mental experience as unscientific.

CLINICAL Involving or based on direct observation of a patient.

COGNITION The process involved in knowing, or the act of knowing, which in its completeness includes perception and judgment.

DEDUCTION In logic, a rigorous proof, or derivation, of one statement (the conclusion) from one or more statements (the premises).

EMPIRICAL Originating in or based on observation or experience.

EPIGENETICS The study of the molecular mechanisms that affect the activity of genes, essentially turning some genes on and others off.

ETIOLOGY Cause or origin, especially of a disease.

GESTALT PSYCHOLOGY A school of psychology founded in the 20th century that emphasizes holistic experiences, in contrast to artificially discrete phenomena such as stimulus and response. It sought to encompass the qualities of form, meaning, and value that prevailing psychologists had either ignored or presumed to fall outside the boundaries of science.

HEURISTIC An intuitive problem-solving method that involves taking certain steps toward the solution of a problem and evaluating the results as these steps are completed.

HYSTERIA A neurosis marked by emotional excitability and a tendency to develop sensory and physical disturbances with no apparent organic basis.

INDUCTION Reasoning from particular instances to a general conclusion.

INHIBITION Conscious or unconscious constraint or curtailment of a process or behaviour, especially of impulses or desires.

MORPHOLOGY The form and structure of an organism or any of its parts.

NEUROLOGY The scientific study of the structure, functions, and disorders of the nervous system.

NEURON A cell with specialized processes that is the fundamental functional unit of nervous tissue.

NEUROSIS Any of various mental and emotional disorders that affect only part of a person's personality, are less serious than a psychosis, and involve extreme or atypical reactions (as abnormal fears, depression, or anxiety) to stress and conflict.

NEUROTRANSMITTER A substance that transmits nerve impulses across a synapse from one neuron to another.

PHOBIA An extreme, irrational fear of a specific object or situation.

PHYSIOLOGY The study of the functions and activities of life or of living matter (as organs or cells) and of the physical and chemical processes involved.

PSYCHOANALYSIS A highly influential method of treating mental disorders, shaped by psychoanalytic theory, which emphasizes unconscious mental processes and is sometimes described as "depth psychology."

PSYCHOSIS A fundamental or severe personality disorder characterized by defective or lost contact with reality and often by delusions and hallucinations.

SOCIOLOGY The science of society, social institutions, and social relationships.

STATISTICS A branch of mathematics dealing with the collection, analysis, interpretation, and presentation of masses of numerical data.

STIMULUS Something that directly influences the activity of a living organism or one of its parts (as by exciting a sensory organ).

TRAIT A distinguishing quality (as of personality or physical makeup).

BEHAVIOURISM

Albert Bandura, *Principles of Behavior Modification* (1969), is a classic in the psychology of behaviour modification based on social learning. The leading figure of behaviourism discusses its nature, methods, and goals in B.F. Skinner, *About Behaviorism* (1974).

COGNITIVE SCIENCE

Jean Piaget, *The Child's Conception of Number* (1952), and *The Origins of Intelligence in Children* (1952), are excellent examples of Piaget's research and thinking. An in-depth illustration of complex learning theories in cognitive science is provided in David E. Rumelhart, G. Hinton, and R.J. Williams, "Learning Internal Representations by Error Propagation," in David E. Rumelhart and James L. McClelland, *Parallel Distributed Processing: Explorations in the Microstructure of Cognition*, vol. 1 (1986).

THOUGHT

Classic studies on thought include John Dewey, *How We Think* (1910, reissued 1998); Jean Piaget, *The Psychology of Intelligence* (1950, reissued 2001; originally published in French, 1947); Gilbert Ryle, *The Concept of Mind* (1949, reissued 2002); and Jerome S. Bruner, Jacqueline J. Goodnow, and George A. Austin, *A Study of Thinking* (1956, reprinted 1986). Robert Thomson, *The Psychology of Thinking* (1959, reissued 1977), discusses experimental approaches to thinking; Robert J. Sternberg and Talia Ben-Zeev, *Complex Cognition: The Psychology of Human Thought* (2001), presents a general introduction to thinking and types of thinking; and Diane F. Halpern, *Thought and Knowledge: An Introduction to*

Critical Thinking, 4th ed. (2003), observes the attainment of reflective judgment. Jacqueline P. Leighton and Robert J. Sternberg (eds.), *The Nature of Reasoning* (2004), is a useful collection of articles; as is Janet E. Davidson and Robert J. Sternberg (eds.), *The Psychology of Problem Solving* (2003).

Theoretical developments include Max Wertheimer, *Productive Thinking*, ed. by Michael Wertheimer, enlarged ed. (1959, reprinted 1982), on Gestalt theory; and Allen Newell and Herbert A. Simon, *Human Problem Solving* (1972), on computer simulation.

Frederic Bartlett, *Thinking: An Experimental and Social Study* (1958, reprinted 1982), treats thinking as a skill, sometimes known as the "information-processing" approach; Lev Vygotsky, *Thought and Language*, trans. and ed. by Alex Kozulin, rev. ed. (1986; originally published in Russian, 1934), offers historical context for Soviet research on the topic; and Alex Kozulin, *Psychological Tools: A Sociocultural Approach to Education* (1998), examines ways in which culture influences thought.

MEMORY

Endel Tulving and Fergus I.M. Craik (eds.), *The Oxford Handbook of Memory* (2000), is an excellent reference work. Alan D. Baddeley, *Essentials of Human Memory* (1999), provides a reasonably comprehensive overview of the psychology of human memory; while Ian Neath and Aimée M. Surprenant, *Human Memory: An Introduction to Research, Data, and Theory*, 2nd ed. (2003), discusses methodologies of memory research. Two versions of formal models of memory are given in two essays found in Kenneth W. Spence and Janet Taylor Spence (eds.), *The Psychology of Learning and Motivation*: one by Gordon Bower, "Multicomponent Theory of the Memory Trace," 1:229–325 (1967); and the other by R.C. Atkinson and R.M. Shiffrin, "Human Memory: A Proposed System and Its Control Processes," 2:89–195 (1968). A comprehensive account of interference in long-term memory is provided by G. Keppel, "Retroactive and Proactive Inhibition," in Theodore R. Dixon and David L. Horton (eds.), *Verbal Behavior and General Behavior Theory* (1968), pp. 172–183.

In contrast to works derived largely from laboratory studies, Alan Baddeley, *Human Memory: Theory and Practice* (1990), harmonizes laboratory studies with actual data from brain-damaged patients and is of value to advanced researchers and undergraduates alike. A balanced examination of memory for traumatic events, including the repressed memory controversy, is provided in Richard J. McNally, *Remembering Trauma* (2003). Daniel L. Schacter, *The Seven Sins of Memory: How the Mind Forgets and Remembers* (2001; also published as *How the Mind Forgets and Remembers: The Seven Sins of Memory*, 2003), organizes a discussion of memory for the layperson around the fallibility of the memory system, with a focus on neuroscientific evidence.

PERSONALITY

Definitions of personality as a psychological concept, with treatment of related issues, are found in the following reference works: Rom Harré and Roger Lamb (eds.), *The Dictionary of Personality and Social Psychology* (1986); Richard L. Gregory (ed.), *The Oxford Companion to the Mind* (1987); Raymond J. Corsini *et al.* (eds.), *Concise Encyclopedia of Psychology* (1987); and Jonathan L. Freedman, *Introductory Psychology*, 2nd ed. (1982).

Major theories of personality are surveyed in Calvin S. Hall and Gardner Lindzey, *Theories of Personality*, 3rd ed. (1978); and in Nathan Brody, *Personality: In Search of Individuality* (1988). Roger Brown, *Social Psychology, the Second Edition* (1986); and Irwin G. Sarason, *Personality: An Objective Approach,* 2nd ed. (1972), review and evaluate contemporary personality studies and research methods. The best presentation of psychoanalytic ideas remains Freud's own, available in many translated selections. The following two, edited and translated by James Strachey, can be recommended: Sigmund Freud, *Introductory Lectures on Psychoanalysis* (1977; originally published in German, 1916–17), and *New Introductory Lectures on Psychoanalysis* (1974; originally published in German, 1933). Gardner Murphy, *Personality: A Biosocial Approach to Origins and Structure* (1947, reissued 1966), integrates views and data that reach across historical epochs and many intellectual disciplines. The theory of cognitive controls and styles is carefully analyzed in George S. Klein, *Perception, Motives, and Personality* (1970).

Discussions of the variety of currently held views on personality, demonstrating a broad interdisciplinary approach, include James F. Masterson, *The Search for the Real Self: Unmasking the Personality Disorders of Our Age* (1988); and Arthur Peacocke and Grant Gillett (eds.), *Persons and Personality: Contemporary Inquiry* (1987). Adaptation of personality in social interaction is explored in Joel Aronoff and John P. Wilson, *Personality in the Social Process* (1985); Alan S. Waterman, *The Psychology of Individualism* (1984); Robert A. Levine, *Culture, Behavior, and Personality: An Introduction to the Comparative Study of Psychosocial Adaptation*, 2nd ed. (1982); Nancy Cantor and John F. Kihlstrom, *Personality, Cognition, and Social Interaction* (1981); and Nancy Cantor and John F. Kihlstrom (eds.), *Personality and Social Intelligence* (1987). Issues of personality development from childhood through adulthood are interpreted in Robert L. Leahy (ed.), *The Development of the Self* (1985); Laurence R. Simon, *Cognition and Affect: A Developmental Psychology of the Individual* (1986); Lawrence S. Wrightsman, *Personality Development in Adulthood* (1988); and Erik H. Erikson, *Childhood and Society,* new anniversary ed. (1985).

INDEX

A

acquisition, and memory, 52–55
Adler, Alfred, 10, 83–84, 114–117
aging, 69–71
amnesia, 45, 68–69
analogical inference, 40, 41
autobiographical memory, 60, 62

B

Bandura, Albert, 89, 135–136
behaviourism, 2–3, 5–6, 7, 16, 17,
    22, 123, 124–125, 133–134
Breuer, Josef, 78,–79, 102–103, 109

C

causal inference, 40, 41
categorical inference, 40, 41
child psychology, 5, 8, 10, 17, 20,
    29, 79, 103, 105, 117, 118,
    126, 127–130, 135–136
chimpanzees, 24, 25, 26
Claparède, Édouard, 26, 68,
    117–118
cognitive science, 6–7, 8–9, 14
cognitivist, theories of thinking, 21
concept attainment, 42–43
conditional reasoning, 38–39
conditioning, 2–3, 8, 22, 106, 123
creative thinking, 43–44

D

declarative memory, 52
developmental psychology, 10
Dewey, John, 26, 105
dysexecutive syndrome, 49–50

E

ego, 82, 111, 112, 127
engram, 56, 64
epigenesis, 84
epigenetics, 12–13, 138
episodic memory, 52, 69
Erikson, Erik, 84–85, 131–133
executive attention, 48–50
extraversion, 6, 8, 83, 118, 120, 121
eyewitness memory, 62–64

F

false memory syndrome, 61–62,
    63–64
field dependence–field indepen-
    dence, 98
Freud, Anna, 20, 126–127
Freud, Sigmund, 3–5, 6, 20, 69,
    78–79, 81–83, 84, 103, 105,
    107–114, 116, 117, 118, 120,
    126
functional fixedness, 35